# FLAGS
## OF THE
# WORLD

# FLAGS OF THE WORLD

### General Editor
## BILL YENNE

MAGNA
BOOKS

Published by Magna Books
Magna Road
Wigston
Leicester LE18 4ZH

Produced by Bison Books Ltd.
Kimbolton House
117 A Fulham Rd.
London SW3 6RL

ISBN 1-85422-437-9

Printed in Hong Kong

**Picture Credits:**
All of the individual flags were drawn by Bill Yenne and Tom Debolski. All the maps were drawn by Tom Debolski. All of the photographs were supplied by the governments of the nations whose flags are depicted, except as follows:
American Graphic Systems Archives:
    36 (top).
Anne SK Brown Military Collection,
    Brown University: 9.
National Army Museum: 10.
Reuters/Bettmann: 18, 33, 36 (bottom).
© Bill Yenne: 1-5, 13, 14, 25, 75, 79.

# TABLE OF CONTENTS

# PREFACE

Somewhere in the mists of prehistory, humankind first selected a special symbol by which a person or tribe could be distinguished from others. These images, which anthropologists call *totems*, became the tribal symbols which over time developed into the emblems distinctive of nations. Eventually these took the form of the insignia from which we derive our flags.

The earliest national symbols were ordinary images or badges wrought in metal, stone or wood, and carried at the top of a pole or spear. Thus, Egypt marched to war beneath the sacred emblems of their gods or the fan of feathers of the pharaohs, while the Assyrian insignia was a circular disc bearing a running bull or two bulls tail to tail. Both of these often also had a small streamer attached to the staff immediately below the device. These were probably the first flags. The Greeks also used symbols of their deities, such as the owl of Athens, or legendary animals, like the Pegasus of Corinth, the Minotaur of Crete or the tortoise of the Peloponnesus. Homer suggests that Agamemnon used a purple veil as a rallying signal.

The sculptures of Persepolis show us that the Persians adopted the figures of the sun, the eagle and the like, which in time were replaced by the blacksmith's apron. For the Romans, the figure of a horse or wolf or other animal was used until a lone eagle was adopted by the emperor Marius. Pliny writes that, in his second consulship, Marius ordered that the Roman legions should have the eagle only as their standard. 'For before that time, the eagle marched foremost with four others, wolves, minotaurs, horses and bears, each one in its proper order. Not many years passed before the eagle alone began to be in advance and the rest left behind in the camp. But Marius rejected them altogether, and since then, there has rarely been a camp of a legion in winter quarters without a pair of eagles.'

Meanwhile, there were other insignia. According to Livy, the Roman vexillum, or cavalry flag, was a square piece of textile material fixed to a crossbar at the end of a spear, often richly fringed, and either plain or with devices, and was undoubtedly a flag. The insignia, which distinguished the allied forces from the Roman legions, were also more or less flags, as may be seen on the columns of Trojan and Antonine, the arch of Titus and in many coins and medals of ancient Rome. Later, the Romans adopted for their auxiliaries the dragon of Parthia, which in time became the standard of the Emperors of the West, and which can be said to be the origin of the golden dragon of Wessex and the red dragon of Wales.

The flag of Denmark dates to the twelfth century and is one of the oldest now in use, but the modern flags of the United States, Britain and France were all adopted around the turn of the nineteenth century.

By the beginning of the twentieth century, most of the flags in use today in Western Europe and the Western Hemisphere were already flying. Most of the present flags of Africa were chosen in the 1960s, and in the 1990s a host of new colors appeared in Eastern Europe and the nations of the former Soviet Union.

8

# THE UNITED KINGDOM

P ossibly the first reference to banners in England is in Bede's description of the interview between King Ethelbert and St Augustine, wherein the saint's followers are said to have borne 'a silver cross for a banner'—clearly showing that banners were then in use, but St Augustine did not have one. Banners of this type were formerly part of the usual ornaments of the altar, and are still largely used to add to the pomp of religious processions.

Ecclesiastical flags were often purely pictorial in character, being actual representations of the Trinity, the Madonna or specific saints. At other times, the religious houses bore heraldic banners, as the chiefs of the church were also temporal lords, as well as spiritual lords. Both temporal and spiritual lords took their places among the fighting men at the head of the retainers they were required to maintain in aid of the national defense. In these cases, the distinguishing banner of each contingent obviously conformed to the banners of the respective lords. Heraldic and political devices on flags soon followed, but even when these came freely into vogue they did not supplant ecclesiastical symbols.

The banners of the original orders of knighthood belong to the religious group. That of the Knights Hospitalers

was a silver cross on a black field, while the Templars carried a banner that was black over white horizontal, which they called Breauset 'because they were fair and favorable to the friends of Christ but black and terrible to his enemies.'

The national banner of England—the red cross of her patron, St George—was for centuries a religious one. In 1245 on St George's Day, Frederick II instituted an order of knighthood and placed it under the guardianship of that soldier saint. Its white banner, bearing the red cross, floated in battle alongside that of the German Empire. On St George's Day in 1350, Edward III of England instituted the Order of the Garter, and by the fourteenth century, the cross of St George was worn as a distinctive mark on a surcoat, over the armor, by every English soldier. Whatever other banners were carried, St George's would always be the first in the field.

Scotland's Cross of St Andrew was shaped like the letter 'X,' representing the two pieces of timber driven into the ground to which the saint was tied. Legend asserts that this form of cross appeared in the sky to Achaius, King of the Scots, the night before the great battle with Athelstan. Having been victorious, Achaius went barefoot to the church of St Andrew and vowed to adopt his cross as the Scottish national emblem.

*Facing page:* **The British naval ensign features the Union Jack in its canton, or corner. The flag is seen here flying over a British warship at Cape Breton Island in 1745.**

The joining of the two kingdoms of England and Scotland—henceforth known as Great Britain—into one entity under the sovereignty of King James, necessitated a new design for the flag to typify this union which would blend together the emblems of the two patron saints. The Royal Ordinance of 12 April 1605 states: 'Whereas some difference hath arisen between our subjects of South and North Britain, traveling by seas, about the bearing of their flags, for the avoiding of all such contentions hereafter, we have, with the advice of our Council, ordered that from henceforth all our subjects of this isle and kingdom of Greater Britain, and its members hereof, shall bear in their maintop the Red Cross, commonly called St George's Cross, and the White Cross, commonly called St Andrew's Cross, joined together, according to a form made by our Heralds, and sent by us to our Admiral to be published to our said subjects.'

The royal banner of Great Britain and Ireland, in its rich blazonry of the lions of England and Scotland and the Irish harp, is a good example of the heraldic flag, while the current Union Jack similarly symbolizes the three components of the United Kingdom by the three allied crosses, two of which are the old crosses of St George and St Andrew, the third being the saltire assigned to St Patrick in the seventeenth century.

On 5 May 1634, however, Charles I restricted the use of the Union Jack to the Royal Navy, and the national flags of England and Scotland were used for public departments and the merchant services. On land, the two kingdoms continued under separate administration and separate flags until 1 May 1707.

Possibly the first mention of the composition of the current Union Jack was made in the Order of the King in Council of 5 November 1800. The immediate use of the flag was required by the royal proclamation of 1 January 1801 which stated: 'Whereas by the First Article of the Articles of Union of Great Britain and Ireland it was declared: That the said kingdoms of Great Britain and Ireland should upon this day, being the first day of January in the Year of our Lord One Thousand Eight Hundred and One, for ever after be united into one kingdom, by the name of the United Kingdom of Great Britain and Ireland, and that the Royal Style and Titles appertaining to the Imperial Crown of the said United Kingdom and its dependencies, and also the ensigns armorial, flags and banners thereof, should be such as we, by our Royal Proclamation under the Great Seal of the said United Kingdom, should appoint . . . and that the Union Flag shall be azure, the Crosses Saltire of St Andrew and St Patrick quarterly, per Altire counterchanged Argent and Gules: the latter fimbriated of the second, surmounted by the Cross of St George of the third, fimbriated as the Saltire.'

Today, the Union Jack remains the flag of the United Kingdom, while the Cross of St George represents England and the Cross of St Andrew symbolizes Scotland. Northern Ireland has flown the Union Jack alone as its flag since 1972 when the British government imposed direct rule. Wales flies the green and white bicolor of Gwynedd upon which is superimposed the Y Ddraig Goch (*the red dragon*) of Welsh Prince Cadwaladr, who died in 1172 after repelling an invasion by Henry II of England. The colors date back to the fifteenth century, but the flag was not adopted until 1958. The Union Jack is, of course, flown throughout the United Kingdom.

**Union Jack**

**England (St George)**

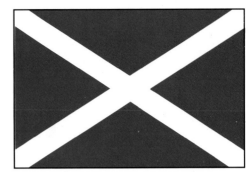

**Scotland (St Andrew)**

**Wales**

**Jersey**

**Guernsey**

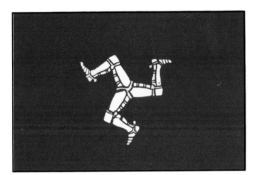

**Isle of Man**

**Bermuda**

**British Virgin Islands**

**Cayman Islands**

**Gibraltar**

**Falkland Islands**

**Hong Kong (until 1997)**

# FRANCE

Officially adopted on 20 May 1794, the present French flag was probably the first vertical tricolor, and thus has influenced the design of countless other flags around the world. It has remained the same for the two centuries since it was first flown, except for a brief period in 1848 when the red and white panels were transposed, although the panels were not *officially* fixed as being of equal width until 1946.

The history of France can be said to have begun with a flag when Clovis (or Chlodwig, from which Ludwig and Louis are derived), dreamt the night before the battle of Tolbiac in 496 that the golden toads in one of his standards had been changed to lilies (*fleurs-de-lis*). In 493, Clovis had married a Christian wife, Clotilda, and during the battle he had vowed that if he were victorious, he would acknowledge her God. The result was the rout of the Alemanni and Clovis' subsequent baptism on Christmas Day. Both he and his wife were buried in the church now known as St Genevieve in Paris.

After his conversion, Clovis used the blue cape of St Martin (which he believed had been the cause of his victory) surmounted with the three gold *fleurs-de-lis*. We should note that St Martin was the Apostle of the Gauls who retired from soldiering to become the Bishop of Tours in 374. His helmet used to be carried by the French in their wars as an incitement to courage, and his cape was originally in the keeping of the monks of the abbey at Marinoutiers, and remained in vogue for some time, but did not always bring victory.

After an interval in which many ensigns were tried, the place of St Martin's was taken by the oriflamme. This oriflamme was the sacred banner of the abbey of St Denis, and had frequently been borne to victory in the struggles of the abbots with their powerful neighbors. The abbey owned the valley of Montmorency and the district known as the Vexin, which is simply a prolongation of that valley down the Seine. Prince Louis (later King Louis the Fat) had been educated in the abbey, and when William Rufus claimed the Vexin and invaded it, Louis, as its Count, marched against him, boldly taking with him the abbot's banner. The effect was immediate, the enthusiasm was boundless. Rufus was defeated, and to secure such desirable results for the future, the oriflamme became the principal flag of France.

The original oriflamme seems to have been a large red banner mounted on a gilt staff with its loose end cut into three tongues resembling flames, between each of which was a green tassel. However, it appears in many other forms, in some of which it is bordered and ornamented with one or more crosses and amulets. It has also been recorded as square in shape: 'The celestial oriflamme so by the French admired, was but of one color, a square red banner.'

The flag retained its preeminence until the time of Charles the Well-beloved, when the English entered Paris and it mysteriously disappeared. At Mons in 1304, Philip the Fair lost it when the Flemings surprised him and carried it off. St Louis lost it in the seventh crusade when he was taken prisoner and the flag became the trophy of his captors. Philip of Valois lost it at Cressy, where, with every other flag, it fell into

*Facing page:* One of the most familiar of all of the world's flags, the simple design of the French Tricolor dates back to 1794. The relative widths of the stripes varied through the years until 1946, when it was decreed by law that they should be of equal width.

the possession of the English. John lost it at Paiders, where the men of the Black Prince dragged it from beneath the corpse of the brave Geoffrey de Charny, the fiftieth of those 'bearers of the oriflamme' to whom it had been entrusted as a sacred charge since the days when Rufus was driven from the Vexin. The last time that it was borne in battle was at Agincourt, on 25 October 1415, when it failed to justify the confidence that was placed in it.

The *fleur-de-lis* was, however, the most commonly used device in the evolution of French imperial symbolism. At the battle of Bouvines, when Philip Augustus defeated the Emperor Otho and the troops of King John, his banner waved as a signal during the critical hour. It consisted of lilies on a blue field. When St Louis returned from his captivity without the oriflamme, he hoisted the lilies on a white field. The *fleur-de-lis* is probably the yellow iris, *Iris pseudacorus*, the 'yellow flag,' so called from its waving in the wind. However, some

authors aver that it is a lance-head—a lance-head in the shape of an iris flower. It was a symbol of royalty long before St Louis took it for his badge when he started for the Crusades. In a miniature of Charles the Fat found in a book of prayers circa 870, the royal scepter ends in a *fleur-de-lis*. The crown of Hugh Capet of 957 in St Denis is formed of *fleurs-de-lis*, as is that of his successors, Robert the Wise (996) and Henry I (1031), and many others. The crown of Uffa, first king of the East Angles in 575, also bears true *fleurs-de-lis*.

St Louis is reported to have been one of those who assert that it is really the *fleur-de-louis*, and in no sense derived from the Belgian river Lys where it once grew in profusion.

Littre, who, ignoring the iris, defined the figure as a heraldic device imperfectly representing three flowers of the white lily joined together. Whatever it may be, it seems to have existed before Clovis, or he would not have seen it in a dream which we need not believe in,

*Below:* **A French sailor hauls down his nation's Tricolor at the end of the day.**

*Facing page:* **A selection of flags from the history of France. The three gold *fleurs-de-lis* are an important icon in French history, and this flag was flown by the Bourbon kings at the time they were overthrown in the 1789 revolution.**

**The *Fleur de lis* flag (c 493)**

**The Flag of Louis XI (1479)**

**The Tricolor (1789)**

though the learned who wrote about the *fleur-de-lis* chose to do so.

During the Hundred Years War, the white cross was used, and white was adopted as France's national color. 'Follow my white plume,' said Henry of Navarre, 'and you will always find it on the road to victory.'

From the time of Louis the Just until the Revolution of 1789, white plumes, scarves and flags were characteristic of French livery. However, sources show that this did not apply to all the flags. Specifically, there is a sky blue cavalry standard in the Museum at the Invalides with the golden sun of Louis XIV, as well as the red and yellow banner of Louis XII, and a red banner with a white cross borne against English invaders.

In 1479, when Louis XI organized the national infantry, he gave them as their national ensign a scarlet flag with a white cross on it. Two hundred years later, the various provincial levies appeared beneath flags of various designs and colors, but all had the white cross as its leading feature.

In 1669, to diminish the confusion, the Minister of Marine issued an order that ensigns were to be blue, powdered with yellow lilies, and have a large white cross in the middle.

When Napoleon was at Auch, in Armagnac, he asked why many of the windows of the cathedral were partially covered with white paper, and was told that they had feared he would be offended at the sight of certain ancient emblems.

'What, the *fleurs-de-lis*?' he replied. 'Uncover them this moment! During eight centuries they guided the French to glory, as my eagles do now, and they must always be dear to France and held in reverence by her true children.'

This was not, however, the opinion of Napoleon's nephew in 1852, when he issued an edict forbidding lilies to be introduced in jewelry, tapestry, or in any other method of decoration, lest they imperil the position of a sovereign whose enemies might use them for political purposes.

The present tricolor began to come into general use in 1789 at the time of the Revolution. It was probably not designed—as has been suggested—with a view of combining the white of the Bourbons with the red of Paris, or the blue of St Martin and the red of St Denis. It was simply the flag of the most flourishing and best known existing republic—the Netherlands—turned 90 degrees.

In the beginning, the tricolor was unofficial, and its adoption was gradual. In 1790, a decree was issued giving to all flags the cravat—a knot of tricolored ribbons at the top of the staff—and on 24 October of that year it was further decreed the color of the national flag next to the staff was to be red, the middle stripe white and the outer blue. Napoleon had serious thoughts of substituting green—which was his favorite color—for the tricolor, but better counsels prevailed, and he turned his attention to the imperial standard, on which he replaced the Bourbon lilies with golden bees.

As we have noted, the tricolor has remained as the flag of France almost continuously for two centuries, and has inspired the adoption of the vertical tricolor for use by dozens of other nations.

# GERMANY

Before there were true national flags anywhere, ships were distinguished by the flags of their ports, and in northern Europe these flags, in the course of time, were gradually replaced by the red and white colors of the Hanseatic League, under which so many of the cities became united. The Hansa was preeminently German and derived its name from *An der See*, (On the Sea). As nations grew, the Hansa declined.

In October 1867, the North German Confederation originated what was to be the first German national flag. It was a horizontal tricolor of black at the top, white in the center, and red at the bottom. The red and white represented the old Hanseatic League, while the black and white came from Prussia.

Thereafter, all of the German states had their own flags. Prussia's was black over white; Pomerania's was blue over white; Baden's was red over yellow; Bavaria's was white over blue; Brunswick's was blue over yellow; Hanover's was yellow over white; Hesse's was red over white; Mecklenburg's was blue, white and red; Saxony's was white over green; Waldeck's was black, red and gold; and Wurttemberg's was black over red. The Teutonic Knights bore the black cross on a white field, which survives in the twentieth century as the Iron Cross—the *Ritterkreuz*—of Germany, which was used by the Kaisers as an insignia. It also saw service as a military symbol and aircraft insignia in West Germany from 1949 to 1991, and has been an important insignia in unified Germany since.

The black, red and gold (*schwarz, rot, geld*) of today's German flag date to flags in use in the Middle Ages, but came to prominence as pan-Germanic colors in the early nineteenth century. They were worn by the Lutzow Free Corps in 1813, and a banner, nearly identical to today's flag, was flown at Hambach in 1832 with the legend *Deutschlands Wiedergeburt* (Germany's Rebirth) emblazoned upon the red band. The same colors were chosen as the flag of the German Confederation of 1848-1852. Even Freidrich Wilhelm of Prussia flew the black, red and gold in Berlin in 1848.

With the rise of the German Empire in the years leading up to 1871 when the First Reich was born, the Prussian red, white and black tricolor came into favor. Preferred by Chancellor Otto von Bismarck, these colors had become the national flag in 1867 and remained so until the end of World War I and the fall of Kaiser Wilhelm's Second Reich in 1919.

The ensign under which the German Navy served in the World War I was white with a black *Ritterkreuz* with a narrow black edging. The cross extended to the edges of the flag, and the upright of the cross was nearer to the flagstaff than to the fly. In the center, on a white circle with a black rim, was the crowned black eagle with the scepter and orb in its talons, and the first quarter was filled with the black, white and red tricolor, charged with the Iron Cross in black with a narrow white edge—the cross of the old Teutonic Knights. The aftermath of World War I, combined with the abdication of the Emperor, brought about drastic changes in German flags.

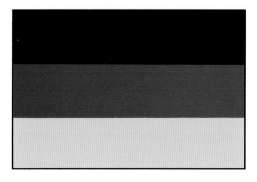

**Germany 1848-1852, 1919-1933 and after 1990**

**Germany, 1867-1919, 1933-1935**     **Germany 1935-1945 (War Flag)**     **Germany 1935-1945**

**Germany (West) 1949-1990**     **Germany (East) 1959-1990**

Accordingly, Article 2 of the Weimar Convention, signed at Schwarzburg on 11 August 1919, decreed that the the federal colors were to be black, red and gold. These federal colors—generally known as the Weimar Colors—were the *schwarz, rot* and *geld* of 1848. The black eagle, or Eagle of the Reich, was also retained, but was shorn of the crown, scepter and the orb.

However, many people resented the Weimar colors as being a reminder of Germany's defeat in the First World War, so the red, black and gold were abolished and the imperial tricolor was reinstated. In the early months of 1933, the rise into power of Adolf Hitler and the National Socialist (Nazi) party brought yet another change in the flags of the Reich. On 2 April 1933, a decree was

issued regarding the flying of flags. The black, white and red tricolor imperial flag, once again the national flag, was to be flown with the Nazi *Hakenkreuz* (swastika) flag. The swastika is in fact an ancient symbol used by many cultures throughout the world to denote the sun, but it was seen by Hitler as being especially symbolic of the Aryan or ancient Germanic values he wished to promote within the context of his vision of German unity. It had previously appeared on flags from the Baltic to the Asian subcontinent to South America, but since the 1933-1945 period, it has come to be thoroughly and completely associated with Nazi Germany.

While it was not adopted as the national flag in 1933, the *Hakenkreuz* flag held a place of almost equal prominence

to the tricolor, and it was decreed that all merchant ships were to fly the black, white and red at the stern, and the *Hakenkreuz* flag on the signal stay or starboard signal yard. In an incident in New York in 1935, a German ship flying the *Hakenkreuz* flag was attacked. The perpetrators were not prosecuted because the courts ruled that the *Hakenkreuz* was a *party* flag not a *national* flag. Thus, in September 1935, Hitler urged the Reichstag to decree the *Hakenkreuz* as the sole national flag of Germany. This was done and the *Hakenkreuz* remained as such until the end of World War II in 1945.

After World War II, Germany was occupied by the four victorious Allied powers and did not exist as an independent state. The international shipping signal flag for the letter 'C' was used on merchant vessels, and old German state flags flew on public buildings not used by the occupying Allied powers who, of course, flew their own flags.

In 1949, the occupation zones of Britain, France and the United States were merged into the new Federal Republic of Germany (*Bundesrepublik Deutschland, BRD*) and the Soviet zone became the Communist German Democratic Repub-

*Above and facing page:* The states of the Federal Republic of Germany and the flags of those states which were part of the Federal Republic prior to reunification in 1990.

*At right:* The national flag of a unified Germany flies before the Reichstag building in Berlin on 3 October 1990.

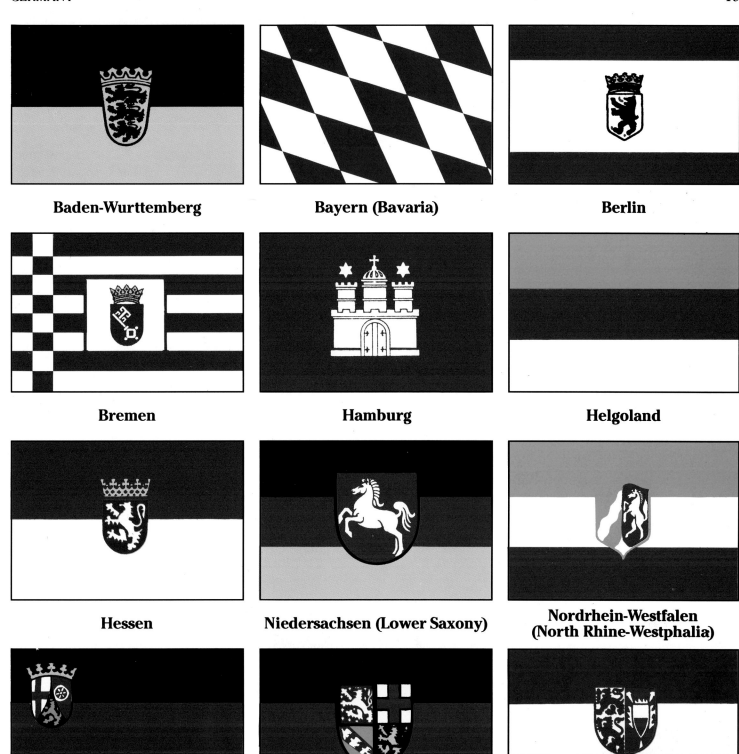

**Baden-Wurttemberg**

**Bayern (Bavaria)**

**Berlin**

**Bremen**

**Hamburg**

**Helgoland**

**Hessen**

**Niedersachsen (Lower Saxony)**

**Nordrhein-Westfalen
(North Rhine-Westphalia)**

**Rheinland-Pfalz**

**Saar**

**Schleswig-Holstein**

lic (*Deutsch Demokratik Republik, DDR*). Both zones returned to the black, red and gold on 9 May 1949, thoroughly rejecting the black, white and red. On 1 October 1959, in order to distinguish itself from the larger and more prosperous BRD (West Germany), the DDR (East Germany) added its hammer and compass coat-of-arms in the center of its flag. This underscored the separation of the two Germanies, which was to remain complete and total for the next 30 years. With the collapse of communism and the fall of the Berlin Wall in 1989, reunification of the two Germanies came swiftly, and the DDR flag was officially retired in October 1990, when Germany once again became a single nation.

# WESTERN EUROPE

The flag of **Andorra** is a tricolor including the colors of the two adjacent countries—blue and red for France and yellow and red for Spain.

One of the world's oldest flags, the flag of **Austria** is a horizontal tricolor of three stripes of red, white and red, which was flown by Leopold V (Heldenthum), the great Hapsburg duke who helped to found the power of Austria in the twelfth century. One of his exploits was the capture of Richard Coeur-de-lion when the latter was on his way home from the Holy Land. Heldenthum's shield now figures as the arms of the Austrian Republic, and the tricolor has been in use intermittently since 1786. It was adopted in its present form from 1921 until 1938—when the Republic of Austria merged with Germany—and was readopted on 1 May 1945, when the Republic of Austria was reestablished.

**Belgium** became an independent kingdom in 1830, having been under the rule of Spain, Austria, France and Holland, and the present flag was adopted on 23 January 1831. Black, yellow and red are the old colors of the provinces of Brabant, Flanders and Hainaut. The tricolor organization is inspired by the French tricolor. Until the early twentieth century, the Royal Standard was the tricolor with the Royal Arms, complete with supporters in the center of the yellow stripe, but today the color of the standard is maroon, with a black shield charged with the golden lion of Brabant, and sur-

*Facing page:* **Flags of the Netherlands fly before the Maritshuis Museum. The Netherlands flag was officially adopted in its present form in 1796, but similar flags, with orange rather than red, predate it by nearly 200 years.**

mounted by the crown of the King of the Belgians. In each of the four corners is the royal cipher—the letter 'B' (for King Baudoin) surmounted by the crown.

Used since 1848 and officially adopted on 21 January 1919, the flag of **Ireland** is a tricolor, with the green being the traditional color of Irish Catholicism and the orange representing the Protestants of Ireland. Orange has been the official color of Irish Protestants since the victory of King William III (of Orange) in the Battle of Boyne (1690). The harp has been the official symbol of Ireland since the fifteenth century, and prior to 1919, the state ensign was a gold harp upon a blue field. This flag is retained as Ireland's presidential flag.

For centuries prior to the mid-nineteenth century, **Italy** was not a nation but an amalgam of independent—and often competing—city-states. Florence, under the Medici, was powerful, as was the Republic of Venice. The Catholic Church, headquartered in Rome, also maintained temporal political control over much of central Italy. Northern Italy had been a republic, the Cisalpine (later Italian) Republic between 1797 and 1802, and its founders had designed the flag for it, a vertical tricolor of green, white and red. The idea was that while giving the new republic a flag of its own, it should closely resemble the flag of France. Curiously, the same tricolor— also because of the French model, was selected by Mexico in 1821 and is still in

use today, albeit with Mexico's own distinctive coat-of-arms. In 1848, the tricolor, which had been withdrawn from use after the downfall of French control of Italy, was hoisted again by the nationalists of the peninsula. It was accepted by the King of Sardinia as the ensign of his own dominion, and included the arms of Savoy.

Savoy had been the nucleus of modern Italy. After the fall of the Kingdom of the Two Sicilies, precipitated by Guiseppe Garibaldi's 1861 invasion, the first national parliament of Italy met at Turin and proclaimed Victor Emmanuel, then the king of Sardinia as the king of Italy. Thus the flag of Naples disappeared, and then Tuscany's red, white and red horizontal flag was hauled down. Parma, Modena, Lombardy and Venice were acquired. The Papal States lowered their yellow and white at Civita Vecchia and elsewhere in 1870, but Vatican City was an independent state, comprised of 108

acres in the center of Rome, was restored to full nationhood in 1929.

It was under the tricolor with the cross of Savoy that Benito Mussolini dreamed of a 'New Roman Empire,' and it was under this flag that Italy joined the Axis in World War II.

When Italy surrendered to the Allies in 1943, Mussolini set up a separate puppet government under German protection called the Italian Social Republic. Under this short-lived republic, the crest of Savoy was replaced on the flag by the fascist fasces (a bundle of rods with an ax in the middle).

After the war, both emblems were deleted, and in 1946 the Italian flag became a simple tricolor.

Red and blue have been used as the **Liechtenstein** national colors since the nineteenth century, but were not officially confirmed until 1921. In 1936, at the time of the Olympic Games in Berlin, the crown was added to the flag to distin-

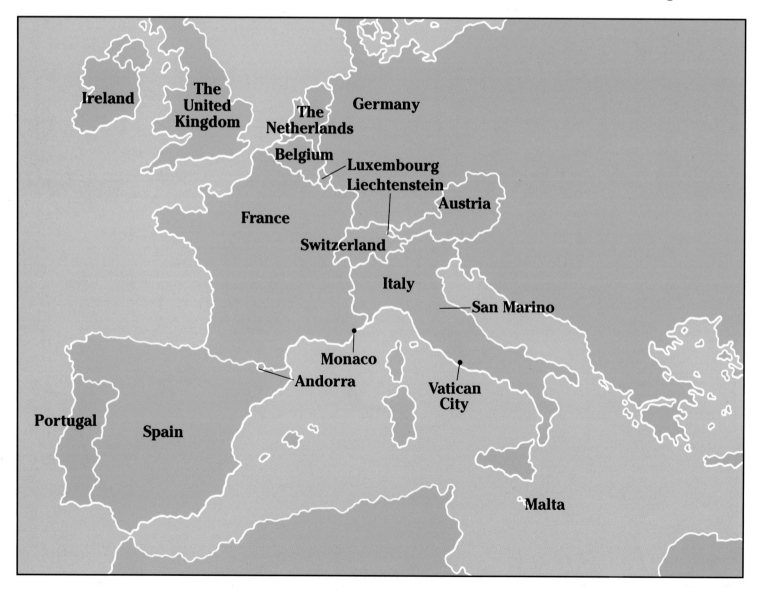

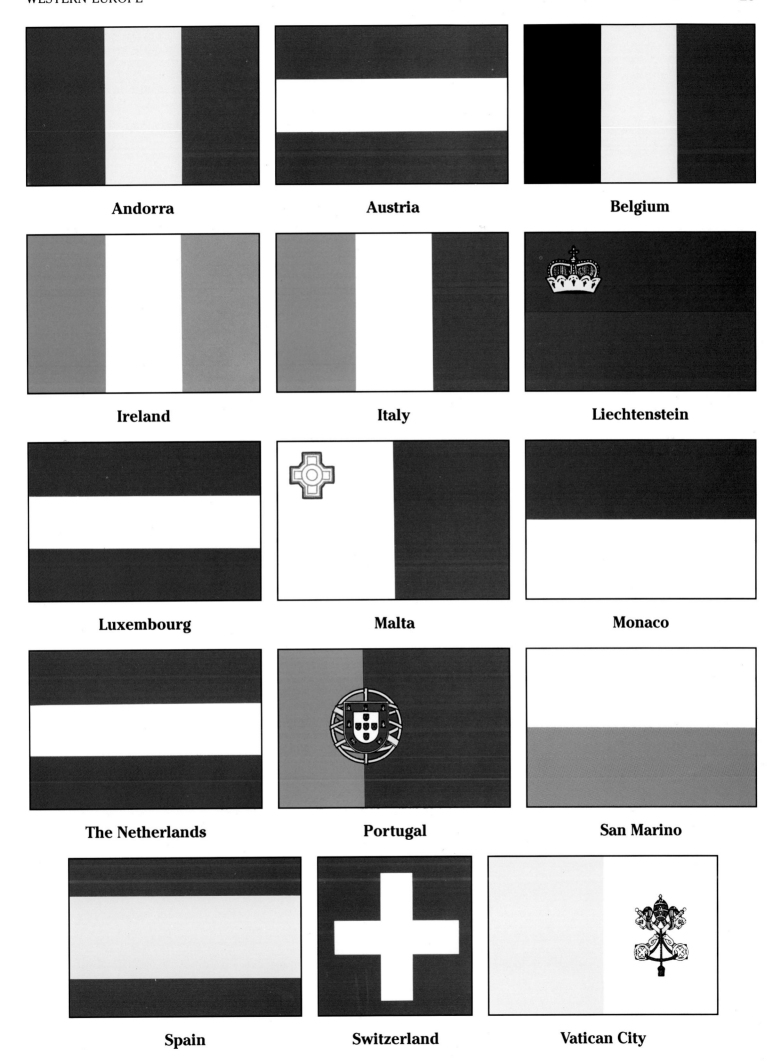

Andorra

Austria

Belgium

Ireland

Italy

Liechtenstein

Luxembourg

Malta

Monaco

The Netherlands

Portugal

San Marino

Spain

Switzerland

Vatican City

guish it from Haiti's, which at that time was identical.

An independent Grand Duchy located in between France, Belgium and Germany, **Luxembourg** formed part of the Germanic Confederation from 1815 to 1866, and the following year it was declared neutral territory. By the Treaty of Versailles after World War I, all its connection with Germany was severed. Luxembourg's flag is a horizontal tricolor of equal stripes of red at the top, white in the center and blue at the bottom. It is identical to the flag of the Netherlands, except for having a lighter blue. The flag was first established on 12 June 1845, but the basic design and colors date back to a banner used by Count Henry IV in 1288.

The colors in **Malta**'s flag may date to the eleventh century, but the Maltese Cross is attributable to the Knights of St John of Jerusalem who ruled this island nation from 1530 to 1798. The cross on the flag is, however, not the Maltese Cross but the George Cross, awarded by Britain's King George VI in 1942 because of Malta's historic resistance to German bombardment in World War II. The British ruled from 1814 to 1964, whereupon the present flag was officially adopted on 21 September 1964.

The national flag of **Monaco** is a red over white bicolor. The colors of this small principality on the Mediterranean date from 1339, but the present flag was adopted officially on 4 April 1881. The Grimaldi family, who have ruled for centuries, fly a white flag with a shield covered with red and white lozenges, supported by monks in brown habits, each brandishing a sword and the motto is 'Deo Juvante.'

**The Netherlands** came into existence as an independent state in 1579, and the Dutch adopted as their flag the colors of William, Prince of Orange, their famous leader—orange, white and blue. At first there was great latitude of treatment, the number of bars of each color and their order being variable, but in 1599 it was officially specified that the flag of the Netherlands was to be orange, white and blue, in three horizontal stripes of equal width. The orange was eventually changed to red in 1796—possibly due to the indefiniteness of the orange and its propensity to fade in the sea air. By 1643, the Dutch flag had become the tricolor

*At right:* Belgian provincial flags fly over the city of Bruges. Seen here (*left to right*) are the flags of Hainaut, Luxembourg (not to be confused with the adjacent, independent Grand Duchy of Luxembourg) and Namur.

which is used at present, although during the French Revolution, the Netherlands became the Batavian Republic under the French. During this time, the naval flag had a figure of Liberty in the upper canton on a white field, but the innovation was not popular, as the sailors preferred the plain tricolor. In 1806, when Louis Bonaparte became king, the figure was deleted. The present horizontal tricolor of red, white and blue has been in use since the sixteenth century and was confirmed by royal decree on 21 September 1806.

**Portugal**, as a republic, retains as its emblem the arms of the monarchy, which was deposed in 1910. These arms are a simple and effective device of the seven castles and five shields. The five blue shields, placed on a shield of white, commemorate the victory of Alfonso Henriquez in 1139 over five Moorish princes at the battle of Ourique, while the five white circles placed on each symbolize the five wounds of the Savior in whose strength he defeated the infidels to become the first king of Portugal. The red border with its seven gold castles was added by Alfonso III after his marriage in 1252 to the daughter of Alfonso the Wise, King of Castille. These arms have remained unaltered for centuries. In the republican emblem the shield is framed in an armillary sphere.

The flag of **San Marino**, a horizontal bicolor of white over blue, is sometimes flown with a representation of the arms. The arms of this small republic on the Adriatic consist of a blue shield, upon which are three green hills, each with a white tower—representing Guaita, Cesta and Montale—with an ostrich feather floating from the battlements. The shield is surrounded with a wreath of oak and laurel, and, strange to say—given this is a republic—the wreath is ensigned with a crown. The arms date to 1797 but the colors originated in the third century.

For centuries, the colors of Imperial **Spain** were red and gold. Probably taken from the arms of Aragon, these were originally four thin, red vertical stripes on a golden ground. The red and gold have been superceded twice in recent memory. The first time was during the 1873-1874 republic when the bottom stripe was changed to purple. After the 1931 revolution, the republic retained the old red and yellow, but again added the purple bottom stripe creating a horizontal tricolor of red, yellow and purple, with the national arms placed in the center of the yellow stripe. In 1936, after the Spanish Civil War, Francisco Franco brought back the old red and gold horizontal tricolor as we see today, but with a different coat-of-arms. The royal arms were reinstated when King Juan Carlos returned to the throne in 1975 but deleted again in 1981.

**Switzerland** chose the simple white cross of the crusaders. In his chronicle, *Justinger the Bearnois*, Gautier says that after speaking to the Swiss forces leaving Berne to march against the coalition of nobles in 1339, Justinger said 'all were distinguished by the sign of the Holy Cross, a white cross on a red shield, for the reason that the freeing of the nation was for them a cause as sacred as the deliverance of the holy places.' In fact, the white cross on red had been the 'Blood Banner' of the Holy Roman Empire. Each of the Swiss cantons also has its own cantonal color. For example, Basel has black and white, St Gall has green and white, Aargau has black and blue, Glarus has red, black and white, Uri has yellow and black, Lucerne has blue and white, Ticino has red and blue, while Geneva and Berne have red and yellow. The Swiss flag is officially square.

The yellow and white flag now used by **Vatican City** was chosen in 1808 by Pope Pius VII as the ensign of the Papal States. It should be noted here that in heraldry, yellow and white are symbolic of gold and silver. The colors were approved in 1825 and flew until 1870 when the Papal States were incorporated into Italy. The rapprochement between the Church and State in Italy in 1929 and the creation of the Vatican State brought out the ancient yellow and white flag of the Papal States again. The crossed keys and crown are symbolic of St Peter's keys to heaven (*Matthew XVI:19*) and of the authority of the papacy. The keys are also rendered in yellow and white to represent gold and silver.

# SCANDINAVIA

In use by Danes since the twelfth century, the present flag of **Denmark** is red, charged with a white cross, the upright of which is placed one-third of the length of the flag from the staff. In 1219, King Waldemar II of Denmark was leading his troops into action against the Livonians. The moment was a critical one, and the King saw, or thought that he saw, a white cross in a red sky, and gladly welcomed such an assurance of divine aid in answer to his prayers. In due course he adopted the white cross on a red field as his country's flag, known as the Danneborg, the name signifying the strength of Denmark. The Danish flag is one of the oldest flags in continuous use and the other Scandinavian flags are based upon its basic design.

The flag of **Finland** is white, with a blue cross, the center of the cross being nearer to the staff than to the center of the flag. It was first adopted in 1863 but not flown over an independent nation for 56 years. For many years Finland was a bone of contention between Sweden and Russia, and was finally ceded to the latter in 1809. It became an independent republic in 1919.

Ruled by Denmark from 1380 to 1918, **Iceland** nevertheless has always been autonomous and linguistically pure. Traditionally, its colors have been blue and white. However, when the Danish-Icelandic Union Act of 30 November 1918 made Iceland an independent kingdom, it added red in deference to the former monarchy. By the royal decree of 12 February 1919, King Christian X of Denmark, reluctantly approved the flag. The last ties with the Danish crown were severed in 1941.

The flag of **Norway** was officially adopted on 17 July 1821 after the country gained its independence from Denmark. The design is that of the Danish flag with a blue cross superimposed. Norway formed a union with Sweden under Swedish kings from 1814 to 1905, but the current flag was flown on land during that time and at sea after 1898.

**Sweden** has flown the yellow cross on the pale blue field since Gustavus Vasa became its king in 1523, but the colors were in use as early as 1364. The present flag was officially adopted on 6 June 1663, an event whose anniversary is celebrated as Swedish Flag Day. The Royal Standard is of the same pattern but is swallow-tailed, and has the horizontal portion of the cross prolonged into a point so as to give the flag three tails. In the center of the flag is a large white square, placed over the center of the cross, which bears the royal arms and supporters upon a pavilion, which is topped with the royal crown.

*Facing page:* **The flag of Sweden is the centerpiece of this changing of the guard ceremony in Stockholm.**

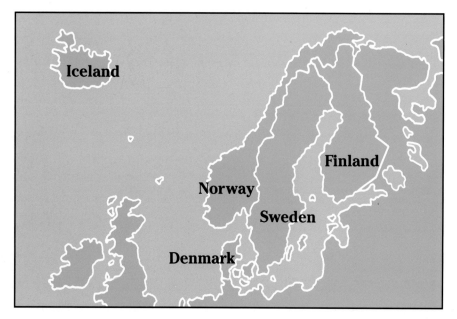

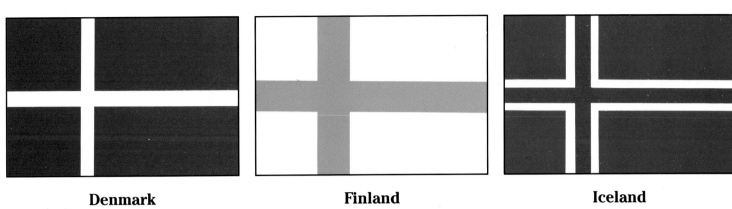

**Denmark**         **Finland**         **Iceland**

**Norway**         **Sweden**

# EASTERN EUROPE

Conquered by the Turks in 1431, **Albania** remained under their domination until 1912, when, by the Treaty of London, it regained its independence. From September 1914—when the first king abdicated—until 1925, when Albania was proclaimed a republic, there was no definite ruler. In 1928, Achmed Zogu, the first president, was declared king. Though it was not officially confirmed until 15 March 1945, a national flag was adopted at that time. It was a deep crimson ensign with the black double-headed eagle of Skanderbeg, the great fifteenth-century Albanian patriot. Skanderbeg chose this emblem because of a very old tradition that Albanians are descendants of an eagle. Shqiperia, or Shgyptar—the Albanian name for the Albanians—means 'descendants of the eagle.' The yellow outline of a star was included above the eagle from 1946 until 1992.

Prior to World War I, **Bosnia-Herzegovina** was dominated by Turkey and later became independent components of the Austro-Hungarian Empire. Sarajevo, Bosnia's capital, had the dubious distinction of being the place where Austria-Hungary's Archduke Franz Ferdinand was assassinated in 1914, thus providing the catalyst for World War I. In 1918, the two nations became states in Yugoslavia. As Bosnia-Herzegovina after 1944, it flew a single state flag based on the national flag of Communist Yugoslavia. In 1991, Yugoslavia began to disintegrate, and in 1992, Bosnia-Herzegovina asserted its independence and began to fly its own non-Communist flag. The Serbian-dominated Yugoslav government went to war in 1992 to prevent Bosnia-Herzegovina's secession.

After the battle of Kossovo in 1389, **Bulgaria** fell under the rule of the Turks, but eventually regained its freedom in 1878. The national flag consists of a plain tricolor of white, green and red, with white symbolizing the country's stand for peace; green, the virtues of an agricultural country; and red for the bravery and gallantry of the Bulgarian army. The flag was modeled on the then-current—and present-day—flag of Russia, which was identical except for its having a blue stripe rather than green. Under Communist rule, the flag bore the nation's arms with a red star in the upper left, but this was provisionally deleted after 1990.

**Croatia** was independent from 1102 until 1849 when it became an autonomous kingdom under the Hungarian Empire. It remained under the domination of the Austro-Hungarian Empire until 1918 when it was merged into Yugoslavia. Croatia was nominally independent under German oversight during World War II, but became part of Yugoslavia again in 1944. As a state within the Communist Yugoslav federation, Croatia flew a horizontal tricolor like today's flag, but with a red star

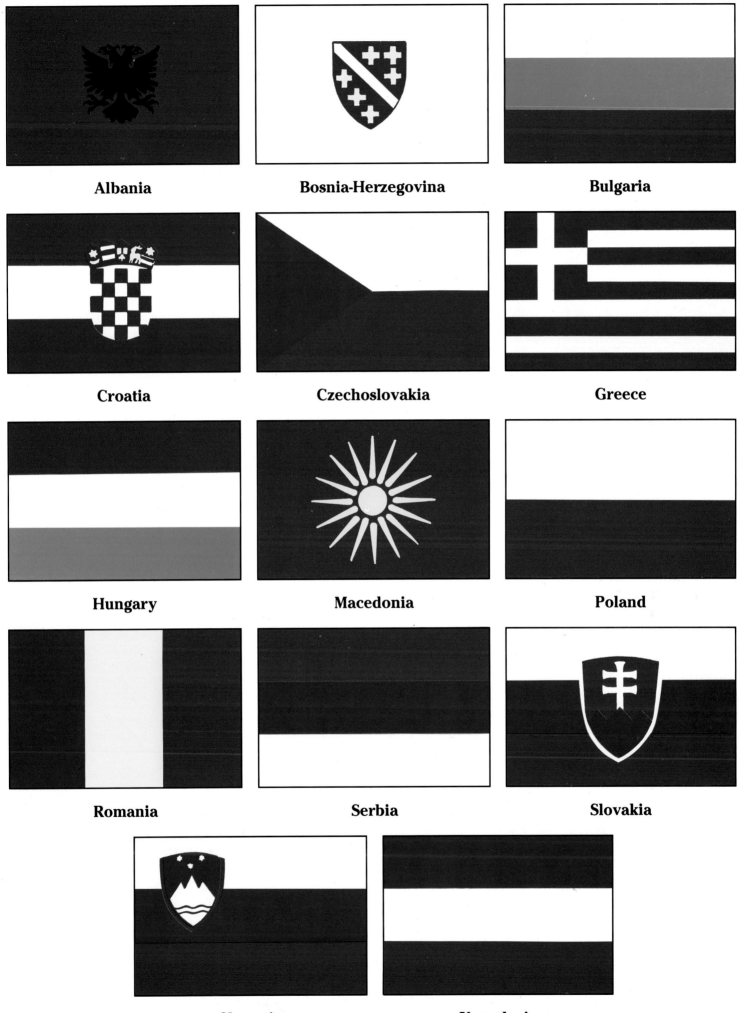

Albania

Bosnia-Herzegovina

Bulgaria

Croatia

Czechoslovakia

Greece

Hungary

Macedonia

Poland

Romania

Serbia

Slovakia

Slovenia

Yugoslavia

instead of the Croatian coat-of-arms. As such, it was nearly the same as the Yugoslav national flag except for the transposition of the red and blue. Croatia seceded from Yugoslavia in 1991 and became independent after a brief but brutal civil war.

When **Czechoslovakia** obtained its independence in 1918, the new nation included the former Austrian provinces of Bohemia and Moravia, as well as **Slovakia**. The flag was established by the law of 30 March 1920. The colors of the ancient kingdom of Bohemia were red and white, and blue was that of Moravia. The Bohemians and Moravians adopted a red and white bicolor in 1918, and the blue was introduced in 1920 to symbolize Slovakia. In July 1992, however, Slovakia voted to withdraw from the Czech republic.

The flag of **Greece** is characterized by nine horizontal stripes, five light blue, four white and a canton of light blue charged with a white cross. Light blue was adopted by the Greek nation as a compliment to the Bavarian prince who became their first king in 1822, but when the Bavarian influence departed and the monarchs came from the Danish house, the light blue became dark blue. With the coming of the Republic in 1924, the blue was again changed and reverted to the pale blue shade. Greece was occupied

by Germany for four years during World War II, and at the end of the occupation in 1944 the monarchy was reinstated. The king was again deposed in 1967, and the flag officially reverted to dark blue on 18 August 1970.

The horizontal tricolor of **Hungary** dates to 1848, but the colors may have originated as early as the ninth century. This flag was superseded by the Austrian colors during the period of the dual monarchy of Austria-Hungary. In 1918, Hungary became an independent kingdom and reverted to its old colors—which, indeed it had never given up—for in the old Austro-Hungarian merchant flag, the right-hand side consisted of the flag and arms of Hungary. Since then, numerous monarchist, fascist and socialist crests have appeared on the white band, but on 1 October 1957 the present flag, with its clean white band, was officially adopted.

The national flag of **Poland** is white over red. Poland was an independent major power from the fourteenth through the seventeenth century, but from 1772 to 1918 it was divided between Russia, Austria-Hungary and Prussia, and obtained its independence again after World War I. Having become independent on 11 November 1918, Poland officially adopted the current flag on 1 August 1919, but these colors have long been associated with Polish history.

Occupied by Rome between 106 and 271 AD, **Romania** was for many years under the domination of the Turks, but eventually obtained its freedom in 1878. In 1918, Romania acquired the Dobrogea, and after the World War I, Bessarabia, Transylvania and Bukovina. The three colors of the current flag date to 1834, and the flag took its present form in 1848. The colors are blue for the sky, yellow (or gold) for wealth and red for bravery. The colors also represent those of Romania's two distinct districts, the red and blue of Moldavia (see also Moldova) and the blue and yellow of Wallachia.

Once independent and later a component of the Austro-Hungarian Empire, **Serbia** emerged in 1918 as the centerpiece of Yugoslavia. Indeed, Belgrade, the capital of Serbia became the capital of Yugoslavia. Long an ally of Russia, Serbia adopted a flag that was the reverse of the pre-1917 and post-1991 Russian flag. In fact, the Serbian colors became the basis of the post-1918 Yugoslav flag and several present flags of former Yugoslav states. Beginning in 1991, when the Yugoslav federation began to fall apart, Serbia went to war against its former federation partners under the Yugoslav flag, treating their wars of independence as a Yugoslav civil war.

Prior to the end of World War I, **Slovenia** was **Carinola**, a province of Austria. In 1918, it became a component of Yugoslavia under a state flag which was identical to the pre-1917 Russian flag. After World War II, when Yugoslavia became Communist, the red star was added to the center. In 1991, Slovenia declared its independence and the centered star was replaced by an offset coat-of-arms.

After World War II, a Communist coat-of-arms was added to the tricolor, but this was a sore point with the populace. During the 1989 revolution, the most commonly seen flag was the tricolor, with a hole literally *cut into* the gold stripe where the offensive coat-of-arms had been. Since 1990, the official flag has been the simple tricolor.

**Yugoslavia** was created in 1918 when the Ottoman and Austro-Hungarian empires were dissolved and Serbia, Montenegro, Bosnia, Herzegovina and Macedonia were united with Croatia and Slovenia. The old Serbian flag had been a horizontal tricolor of red, blue and white, the reverse of the pre-1917 and post-1991 Russian flag. The Yugoslav national flag was the reverse of the Dutch tricolor. On 31 January 1946, after World War II and the Nazi occupation, the Communists under Josip Broz Tito consolidated control over all of Yugoslavia, and a large red star was added to the flag. When civil war began in 1991, Yugoslavia crumbled and the pre-1918 components emerged as independent nations with individual flags. By the time that Yugoslavia was expelled from the United Nations in 1992, Serbia was the only major component left in the former Yugoslavian federation.

# THE NATIONS OF THE FORMER USSR

**Union of Soviet Socialist Republics (1922-1991)**

Prior to the overthrow of Tsar Nicholas II in 1917, Imperial **Russia** had possessed a multitude of flags, prominent among which were the imperial standards of yellow, charged with the black double-headed eagle, which date back to 1472 when Ivan the Great married Sophia, a niece of Constantine Palaeologus and assumed the arms of the Greek Empire. Similar to today's national flag, the merchant flag had a horizontal tricolor of three equal stripes of white at the top, blue in the center and red at the bottom. Another well-known flag was the white flag with the blue saltire Cross of St Andrew.

The present Russian flag was adopted in 1799 as a civil flag to accompany the two-headed eagle imperial flag of the tsar. However, the general form of the flag actually dates to 1699 when Tsar Peter I himself designed a flag that was identical except for the superimposition of a gold imperial eagle on the blue band. The colors represent (*from top*) the 'White Russians' (Byelorussians), the 'Lesser Russians' (Ukrainians) and the 'Great Russians.' The imperial livery colors, incorporated into a horizontal tricolor consisting of (*from top*) black, orange and white, saw service as a civil flag from 1858 to 1883, but were quite unpopular. Therefore, the white, blue and red tricolor served as Imperial Russia's civil flag from 1799 to the Revolution in 1917. Although the imperial eagle flag was banned immediately, the tricolor was adopted briefly as the flag of the new Russian Republic. By 1922, however, it had been replaced by the red Communist flag of the USSR.

The tricolor remained dormant, but not forgotten. In August 1991, when Russian President Boris Yeltsin declared an end to the USSR, the old tricolor suddenly reappeared everywhere, and by the end of the year it had replaced the red Soviet flag on all public buildings.

Between 1922 and 1991, the **Union of Soviet Socialist Republics (USSR)—**

which superseded the old tsarist Russian Empire—consisted of up to 16 republics, each of which had its own flag. After the overthrow of the tsar in the 1917 Revolution, a Russian Republic was formed briefly but it collapsed under the weight of a civil war in which the Communists under Vladimir Lenin seized power. After long discussion over what form the new government of the former Russian Republic would take, the Union of Soviet Socialist Republics was officially created on 30 December 1922.

The national flag of the USSR from 1922 to 1991 was red with a yellow (gold) hammer and sickle device in the canton. It took precedence over all the flags of the constituent republics, all of which were also primarily red, with the hammer and sickle.

In 1991-1992, the red flag of the USSR was officially retired, and all the constit-

uent republics—except Tajikistan and Kazakhstan—revived the flags which they had flown prior to being incorporated into the Soviet Union.

When it officially came into being in 1922, the Union contained four Soviet Socialist Republics (SSR): the **Russian Federated SSR**, the **Ukrainian SSR**, the **Byelorussian SSR** and the **Transcaucasian SSR**.

The **Ukraine** and **Byelorussia**, along with Russia were the basic Slavic republics of the USSR. The Ukraine—the original Cossack state of the thirteenth to seventeenth century—joined with the Muscovites in 1654 and was part of the Russian Empire until 1918, after which it was independent under its own flag for four years before becoming one of the first SSRs. Being a land of open plains, Byelorussia (White or free Russia) always had nebulous borders that

*Above:* **A young army recruit takes an oath of loyalty to Russia. When this photograph was taken in 1991, the Russian flag had replaced the former Soviet flag (*seen opposite*), but the accoutrements of the uniforms still bore Soviet symbols such as the once-omnipresent hammer and sickle.**

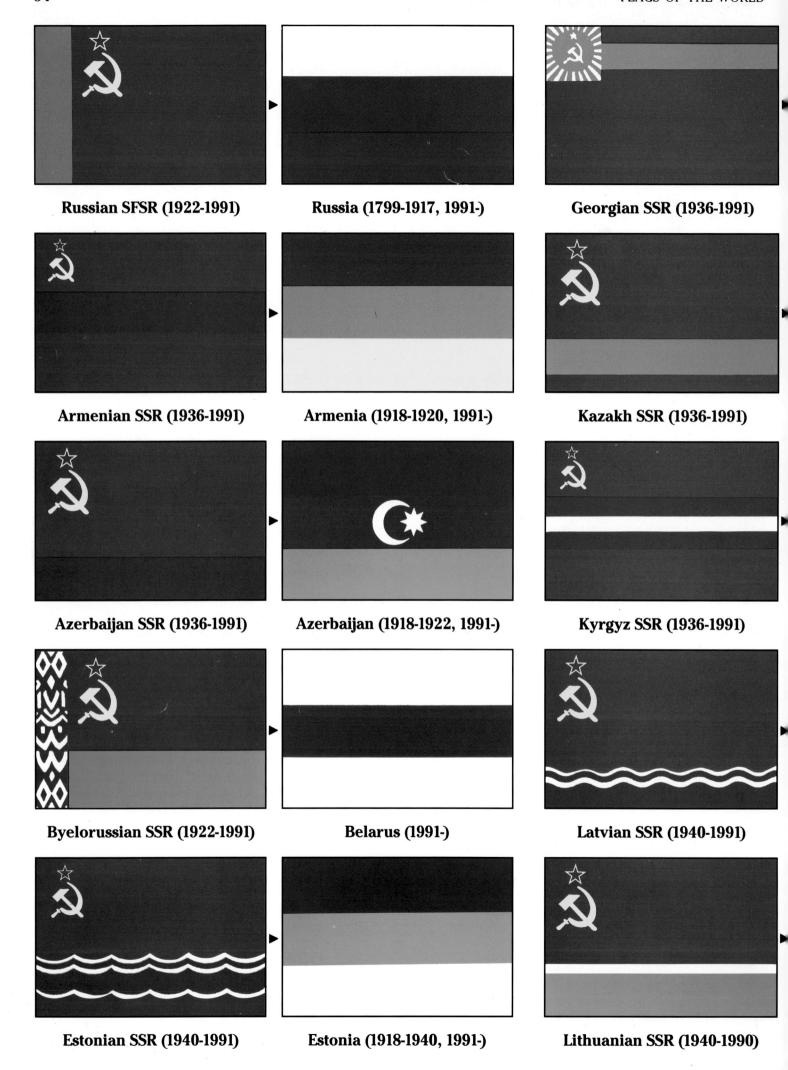

**Russian SFSR (1922-1991)**   **Russia (1799-1917, 1991-)**   **Georgian SSR (1936-1991)**

**Armenian SSR (1936-1991)**   **Armenia (1918-1920, 1991-)**   **Kazakh SSR (1936-1991)**

**Azerbaijan SSR (1936-1991)**   **Azerbaijan (1918-1922, 1991-)**   **Kyrgyz SSR (1936-1991)**

**Byelorussian SSR (1922-1991)**   **Belarus (1991-)**   **Latvian SSR (1940-1991)**

**Estonian SSR (1940-1991)**   **Estonia (1918-1940, 1991-)**   **Lithuanian SSR (1940-1990)**

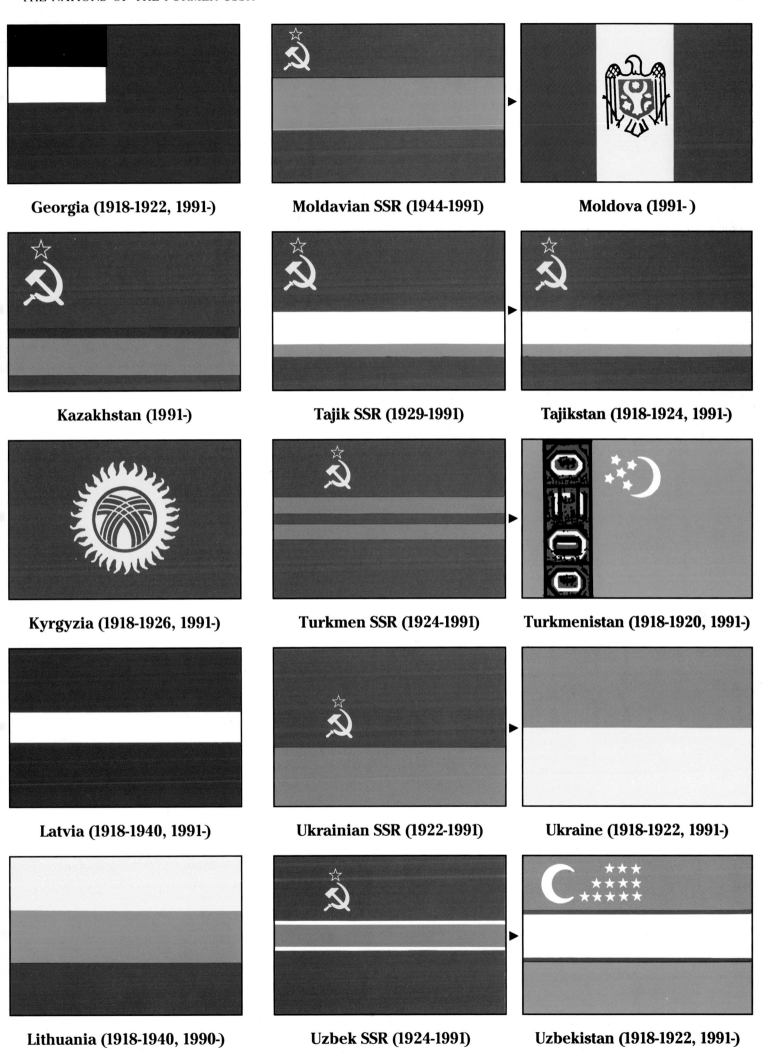

**Georgia (1918-1922, 1991-)**

**Moldavian SSR (1944-1991)**

**Moldova (1991- )**

**Kazakhstan (1991-)**

**Tajik SSR (1929-1991)**

**Tajikstan (1918-1924, 1991-)**

**Kyrgyzia (1918-1926, 1991-)**

**Turkmen SSR (1924-1991)**

**Turkmenistan (1918-1920, 1991-)**

**Latvia (1918-1940, 1991-)**

**Ukrainian SSR (1922-1991)**

**Ukraine (1918-1922, 1991-)**

**Lithuania (1918-1940, 1990-)**

**Uzbek SSR (1924-1991)**

**Uzbekistan (1918-1922, 1991-)**

shifted periodically between Russia, Poland and Lithuania. Part of the Russian Empire until 1918, Byelorussia lost much of its territory to Poland in 1921, regained it in 1939 and then was occupied by Germany in 1941-1944. Ukraine and Byelorussia were the only Soviet Republics to become members of the United Nations in the 1945-1991 period. The USSR itself was, of course, also a United Nations member. In 1992, its seat was

*At right:* Soviet soldiers raise the flag of the USSR over the Reichstag in Berlin, which was captured by Red Army troops in May 1945.

*Below:* Flanked by the Russian flag, President Boris Yeltsin speaks to the Russian parliament.

transferred to the Russian Republic and the other former Soviet republics were admitted to the United Nations.

Also formed in 1922, the **Transcaucasian SSR** was an amalgam of **Armenia**, **Azerbaijan** and **Georgia**. Part of the Turkish (Ottoman) and Russian empires before World War I, these three states became independent under their own flags in May 1918. They were, however, occupied by the Russian Communists and forged into a single SSR in 1922. On 5 December 1936, the Transcaucasian SSR was dissolved, and the three constituent parts became the Armenian SSR, the Azerbaijan SSR and the Georgian SSR. They became independent in 1991 and once again raised their 1918 flags.

In Central Asia, five Islamic nations were annexed by the Russian Empire during the nineteenth century: **Kazakhstan**, **Kyrgyzstan**, **Tajikistan**, **Turkmenistan** (part of ancient Turkistan) and **Uzbekistan**. These colonies were quickly seized by the Communists after the Revolution, and in 1922 they became part of the Russian Federated SSR. They were in turn spun off as SSRs, the Uzbek SSR and Turkmen SSR in 1924, the Tajik SSR in 1929 and the Kazakh SSR and Kyrgyz SSR in 1936. When these republics became independent in 1991, Uzbekistan and Turkmenistan adopted flags carrying the Islamic crescent, while Kazakhstan and Tajikistan remained the only nations of the former USSR to retain the old hammer and sickle motif.

**Moldavia** was part of the region known as Bessarabia that has historically shifted between Romania, Turkey and the Russian Empire. The Russians seized the area from Turkey in 1812, Romania gained part of it in 1918 after World War I, and in 1924 the remainder was merged into the Ukrainian SSR until 1940. The Moldavian SSR was established on 2 August 1940 and the country became independent 51 years later as **Moldova**, adopting at that time a flag that was strikingly similar to that of Romania (*see Romania*).

**Estonia** is the most northerly of the Baltic republics, and it obtained its independence in 1918, with a republic being proclaimed in February of that year.

Between 1940 and 1991, Estonia and its Baltic neighbors were not independent, and were considered to be 'republics' within the USSR. The flag used between 1918-1940 was officially readopted in 1991. The colors date as far back as 17 September 1881 when they were chosen by the first Estonian Students' Association. It is generally understood that their significance is blue for the sky, mutual confidence and fidelity; black for the nourishing soil, the dark past of the country and the 'Melanchlaeni of Herodotus.' (These black-cloaked people of the north mentioned by the Greek biographer Herodotus are supposed to have been the ancestors of the Estonians.) White represents the snow—the color of Estonia during the winter months—and hope for the future and moral cleanness.

**Latvia** became an independent republic when it obtained its freedom from the tsarist Russian Empire in 1918. The national flag, which was adopted, was crimson with a white horizontal strip. The Soviet Union occupied Latvia, along with Lithuania and Estonia, in 1940, and all three remained Soviet 'republics' until the dissolution of the USSR in 1991.

At that time, Latvia readopted its 1918-1940 flag.

**Lithuania** also became an independent republic when it obtained its freedom from the tsarist Russian Empire in 1918. The Soviet Union swallowed Lithuania, along with Latvia and Estonia, in 1940, and it remained a Soviet 'republic' until its declaration of independence from the USSR in 1990. Prior to 1940, and again after 1990, the state flag was scarlet, with a design of a mounted knight in armor on a white horse, the latter being caparisoned in red. On the red shield borne by the knight (Vytis) there was a double-barred cross in gold, the symbol of endurance. The origin of the knight is unknown, though historians maintain that the princes of Lithuania used this device upon their banners as early as the twelfth century, when it was known as a symbol of valor. The knight was also used on seals by Vytautas and other grand dukes of Lithuania. On the reverse side of the standard there was a design in white which represented the Gates of Gediminas (Gedimino stulpai), symbolizing the expansion of Lithuania during the thirteenth century.

*Above:* **The 15 constituent republics of the USSR became 15 separate, independent and quite dissimilar nations in 1991.**

# THE
# MIDDLE EAST

Until the end of World War I and the collapse of the Ottoman Empire, the entire Middle Eastern region—except Iran (Persia)—had been under the red flag of Turkey for the better part of a millennium. The early flags of the region, such as those of Syria, Iraq and Jordan, thereafter became horizontal tricolors of black, green and white with red triangles at the left. Only Jordan retains this flag today. There are several interpretations of the meaning of these colors. One is that the red represents the pre-Islam Arab color, green the Islamic color, black the color adopted by the Shiites and white possibly for the conquest of Andalucia by the Arabs. Another explanation is that red represents the blood of the Arabs' enemies, green the fertility of Arab lands, black the fate in store for the Arabs' enemies and white represents Arab nobility and chivalry.

Though the flag was officially confirmed in 1933, the flag of **Bahrain** dates to the 1820 treaty between Britain and the Persian Gulf states which provided for these states to carry a red flag without letters, but with a 'border of white.' Red is the traditional color of the Kharijite peoples of the Persian Gulf region.

Officially adopted on 16 August 1960 at the time of independence from Britain, the flag of **Cyprus** carries a map of this Mediterranean island nation, together with the olive branches symbolizing peace between the Greek and Turkish segments of the population, which has rarely been achieved. Since the Turkish invasion in 1974, the Cypriot flag is usu-ally superseded by those of Greece and Turkey.

The horizontal tricolor of **Iran**, with its three equal stripes, is the reverse of the flag of Hungary. Iran (formerly Persia) has had many flags in its history, several featuring the imperial badge of the lion and the sun, surmounted by a crown. There were two patterns of this badge of the lion and the sun. In one, the lion was seen standing and holding a sword in its right paw, while in the other he was lying down and had no sword. After the fall of the monarchy in 1979, the Persian lion was replaced by the sword and crescents of the Islamic Republic of Iran.

The Turks were driven out of **Iraq** during World War I by the British Mesopotamian Expeditionary Force, and Great Britain was eventually given the mandate for the administration of the country, although Iraq flew its own flag. The green of both the Jordanian and Iraqi flags was transposed with the white band in 1920, and in the 1960s all the horizontal tricolors of the Middle East (except Jordan) replaced the green band with black. In October 1932, Iraq was admitted to the League of Nations and became an independent state. The present flag was officially adopted on 31 July 1963. The three green stars stand for the intended union with Syria and Egypt as the United Arab Republic, which failed to materialize.

The flag of **Israel** is based on the *tallis*, or Jewish prayer shawl, with the Star of David centered on it. The flag was chosen in 1897 by the World Zionist Organization meeting in Basel, and was

Bahrain

Cyprus

Iran

Iraq

Israel

Jordan

Kuwait

Lebanon

Oman

Qatar

Saudi Arabia

Syria

Turkey

United Arab Emirates

Yemen

officially adopted by the state of Israel on 12 November 1948.

The flag of **Jordan** is a horizontal tri-color of black, white and green, black on top and green at the bottom, with a red triangle charged with a white seven-pointed star. This star stands for the seven basic verses from the Koran. This flag is closer to that of the original Arab revolutionary flag of 1918 than any other Arab flag. Both Syria and Iraq had similar flags until 1920 and 1959, respectively.

Carved from the Ottoman Empire, administered by Britain and claimed by Iraq, **Kuwait** became an independent monarchy in 1961 and one of the richest oil sheikdoms in the Middle East within a decade. The flag, in typical pan-Arab colors, was officially adopted on 24 November 1961 and has been in use continuously since, except for a brief period in 1990-1991 when Kuwait was a province of Iraq.

The flag of **Lebanon** is derived from the red and white of the ruling families dating back to the seventh century, and from the Cedar of Lebanon insignia used by the Maronite Christians of Lebanon in the eighteenth century. Following World War I, when Lebanon was a French mandate, the national flag was the French tricolor with a cedar tree in the center. The present flag was adopted on 7 December 1943.

The sultanate of **Oman** originally flew a red flag as detailed in the Treaty of 1820 with Britain. Added later, the arms actually date from the eighteenth century. The white represents peace and the imam, or religious leader. The green represents the fertility of the Green (Diebel al Akhdar) Mountains and refers to the holy pilgrimage of Islamic peoples to Mecca. The present flag was adopted on 17 December 1970.

The flag of **Qatar** was first adopted in 1949, but dates back to 1855. Red and white are the traditional colors of the Kharijite peoples, and this has resulted in the similarity between the Bahrain and Qatar flags. Qatar chose to use a dark maroon rather than red to avoid confusion.

The flag of **Saudi Arabia** is green with the inscription in Arabic 'La Illaha Illa Allah Wa Muhammad Ur-Rusul Ullah,' meaning 'There is no god but God, and Mohammed is the Prophet of God.' Beneath this inscription is a sword in white. When World War I broke out, the Hejaz—a thin slice of territory along the northern part of the Arabian coast of the Red Sea, in which lie Mecca and Medina, the holy places of Islam—was under the dominion of the Turkish Ottoman Empire. In 1916, Sherif Hussein led a revolt, and, with British assistance, threw off Ottoman control. In 1926, however, his neighbor on the east, Ibn Saud, the Sultan of Nejd, whose dominions covered the central part of the Arabian Peninsula and extended to the coast of the Persian Gulf, attacked and conquered the Hejaz and drove out the Sherifian dynasty. Ibn Saud then assumed the title of king and the nation took the name of *Saudi* Arabia. The flag was officially adopted on 30 March 1938, although the single sword was briefly superseded by a pair of crossed swords.

**Syria** was liberated from Turkish domination by British, French and Arab troops in 1918, and Syria and Lebanon were placed under French mandate. In 1930, the latter established Syria as a republic. A new flag was designed and unfurled for the first time on 11 June 1932. It was similar to the current flag, except that the top band was green and the stars were red. The green represents the Abbasid, the white the Fatimid and the black the Omayyad dynasties, respectively. The green was replaced by red in 1958-1961 and permanently in 1963. In 1972, Syria, Egypt and Libya adopted identical flags with the hawk of Quraish on the white band, but this was soon replaced by the stars on Syria's flag.

Once flown over most of the Middle East, the flag of **Turkey** is red with a white crescent whose horns are pointing towards the right. Beside the crescent on the right is a white five-pointed star. The crescent is more a symbol of Constantinople than of the Turks and dates from the days of Philip of Macedonia, the father of Alexander the Great. When Philip besieged Byzantium in 339 BC, he was repulsed time and again, so as a last resort, he attempted to undermine the city walls. However, the crescent moon shone so brightly that his plan was discovered and the city saved. The Byzantines then adopted the crescent as their badge and Diana (goddess of the hunt and of the moon), whose emblem it was, as their patroness. When the Roman emperors came, the crescent was not displaced, and it continued to be the city badge under the Christian emperors. In 1453, when Mohammed took Constantinople under his plain red banner, he availed himself of the old Byzantine badge, declaring that it meant Constantinople on a field of blood.

More than a century before the city fell, the Sultan Othman, founder of the Ottoman dynasty, had had a dream in which he saw a crescent moon growing larger and larger until it covered the horizon from the east to west. This led him to adopt the symbol—which had been that of the Janissaries for at least 50 years previously and also represented Constantinople. Even today, in Moscow and other Russian cities, the crescent and the cross can be seen combined on the churches denoting the Byzantine origin of the Eastern rite. A star within a crescent was also the badge of Richard I more than 250 years before Constantinople fell, which implies that the crescent was adopted by the Saracens, as the device was emblematic of the Crusades and the star stood for the star of Bethlehem. In his badge Richard placed the crescent on its back and the star above it. However, when Islam became triumphant, the Turks took the star and placed it with the upright crescent where the dark area of the moon should be. The old personal flag of the Sultan—the Royal Standard—displayed the 'tughra' consisting of the Sultan's name, the title 'khan' and the epithet 'El Muzaffar Daima,' or 'the ever victorious.' The present Turkish flag differs little in design from that used in the days of the Sultan. After the armistice in 1918, nationalist Turkey, under Mustapha Kemal, changed the color of the flag to green, but this was short-lived, and when the republic came into being, the red color was reinstated, receiving official confirmation on 5 June 1936.

The flag of the **United Arab Emirates** was officially adopted on 2 December 1971. It uses the pan-Arab colors, although the seven constituent emirates all had traditional red flags with white borders or decoration.

**Yemen** flies a horizontal tricolor composed of the traditional pan-Arab colors that was adopted on 1 November 1962. Between 1967 and 22 May 1990 the eastern portion of this Arab nation existed as a socialist 'peoples' republic. The flag in use there was also a horizontal tricolor, but it carried a blue triangle with a red star on the hoist.

# NORTH AFRICA

The present flag of **Algeria** dates to that designed in 1928 by the nationalist leader Messali Hadj, who headed the movement to oust the French colonialists. The flag was adopted in 1954 by the Front for National Liberation and became the flag of an independent Algeria on 3 July 1962. The green represents Islam, the white purity and the traditional Islamic star and crescent motif are rendered in red to represent the blood shed in the war of independence.

Prior to 1914, while **Egypt** was under Turkish rule, its flag was red and bore three decrescents, each of which had a white five-pointed star within the horns, all in white. (A decrescent is the heraldic name for a crescent with its horns pointing to the right.) At that time, with its change of status, Egypt altered its flag to green, and one decrescent took the place of the three white decrescents, with the three white stars retained. The colors of the present flag are those of the Arab Liberation flag, and were adopted when the monarchy was overthrown in 1952. The red represents the revolution, the black represents Egypt's dark past and the white represents its bright

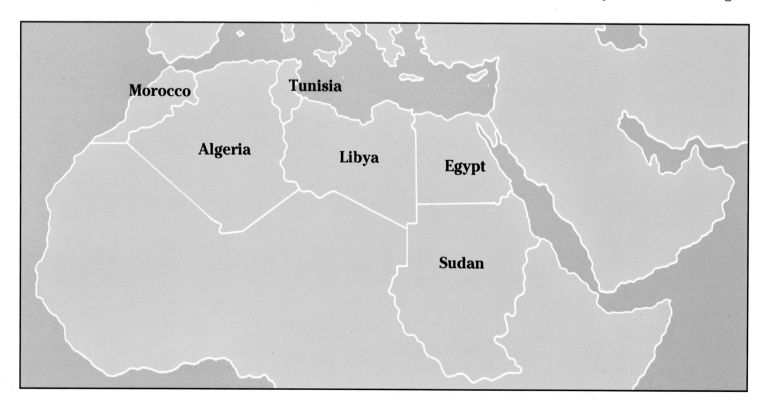

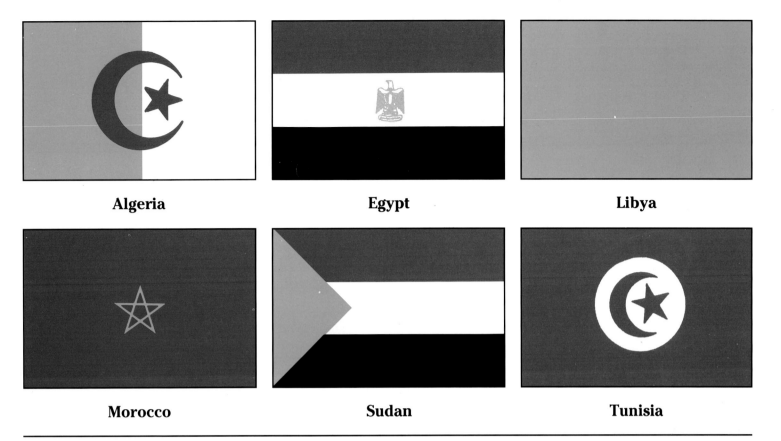

| Algeria | Egypt | Libya |
| --- | --- | --- |
| Morocco | Sudan | Tunisia |

future. In January 1972, the Hawk of Quraish was added. Syria briefly adopted an identical flag when the two nations (along with Libya) were known as the United Arab Republic and later the Federation of Arab Republics, but Syria deleted the hawk from its flag.

Although dominated by Europeans—especially Italians—for the first half of the twentieth century, **Libya** has had a wide variety of flags. In 1947, the black (with white star and crescent) flag of the Senusi sect was recognized by the British. In 1950, this flag was modified to incorporate the pan-Arab colors, and following the 1969 revolution a flag similar to Egypt's was chosen. In January 1972, Libya, Egypt and Syria formed the Federation of Arab Republics and all three adopted identical flags. In 1977, strongman Colonel Muamar Khadaffi withdrew Libya from the Federation because of Egypt's insistence on peace with Israel, and selected the all-green flag of his own sect, giving Libya the only flag in the world that is composed of a single, unadorned color. The color is a traditional Islamic color and also a favorite of Khadaffi.

Like many other Arab nations, **Morocco** used a solid red flag in the nine- teenth century, but added a green penta- gram in 1915. However, Morocco was dominated by the French from 1912 to 1956, so the present flag did not fly over an independent monarchy until the lat- ter date.

The flag of the **Sudan** incorporates the traditional pan-Arab colors of its neigh- bors. This horizontal tricolor was adopted on 20 May 1970, replacing a green, yellow and blue tricolor adopted in 1956.

The current flag of **Tunisia** consists of a field of red with red on a white disc in the center, a red crescent and red five- pointed star. The similarity to Turkey's flag is obvious and not accidental. Prior to the collapse of the monarchy in 1956, the Sultan's flag was a standard of hori- zontal yellow and red stripes, 13 in all, a broad green one in the middle, with six in a group over it and six under it, the upper stripes being yellow and red and the lower being red and yellow. Every yellow one had five black and red cres- cents and four red mullets alternately, and every red one had four green cres- cents and five white mullets, all the mul- lets having the central perforation which marks them as rowels and not stars.

# AFRICA

The flags of Africa tend to feature the color green, which is representative of the fertility of the land. Most flags feature two or three of the three pan-African colors: red, yellow and green. The pan-African colors are those of the flag of Ethiopia, which had been one of the only independent black African nations prior to 1960.

Some African flags are derived directly from those of the original independence movements, while others are adapted from the French tricolor.

The current flag of **Angola** is based on the pre-1975 flag of the Popular Movement for the Liberation of Angola and replaced the Portuguese flag after independence on 11 November 1975. The red symbolizes the blood shed in the struggle for independence. The insignia is based on the old hammer and sickle of the USSR.

Having become independent on 1 August 1968, the former French colony of Dahomey changed its name to **Benin** in 1975. Prior to 1972, the flag was in the pan-African colors. A socialist state from 1972 to 1989, Benin still retains a red star on its otherwise green flag.

The blue of the **Botswana** flag represents rain, which Prime Minister Dr Seretse Khama described as the nation's lifeblood. The black and white 'zebra' stripe represents unity between races. The flag was adopted on 30 September 1966 at the time of independence.

The flag of Upper Volta was originally a black, white and red horizontal tricolor, but the present flag, with pan-African colors, was adopted in 1984 when the country became **Burkina Faso**.

The colors of the **Burundi** flag represent peace (white), hope (green) and the struggle for independence (red). The three stars represent the motto 'Unity, Work, Progress.' The flag was adopted following establishment of Burundi as a republic in 1967.

Although the flag of **Cameroon** was officially raised by an independent nation on 1 October 1961 after independence from France, it had actually been adopted in 1957 under the auspices of the French. It was originally a French-style tricolor with pan-African colors, but two gold stars were added when British Southern Cameroons merged into the nation in 1961. The single star, signifying unity, was adopted in 1975.

The island nation of **Cape Verde** won its independence from Portugal in July 1975 and adopted a flag in the traditional pan-African colors.

Officially adopted on 1 December 1958, the flag of the **Central African Republic** combines the colors of the French tricolor with the pan-African colors. The band of red, the color common to both schemes, binds the others and symbolizes unity, and the red represents the blood of humanity. It has flown continuously except for the 1977-1979 period when then-president Jean Bedel Bokassa declared himself Emperor Bokassa I.

Adopted on 6 November 1959, the flag of **Chad** is based in part on the French tricolor and in part on the pan-African colors. The substitution of blue for the pan-African green is seen as symbolic of the sky and the hope of the rain needed for agriculture.

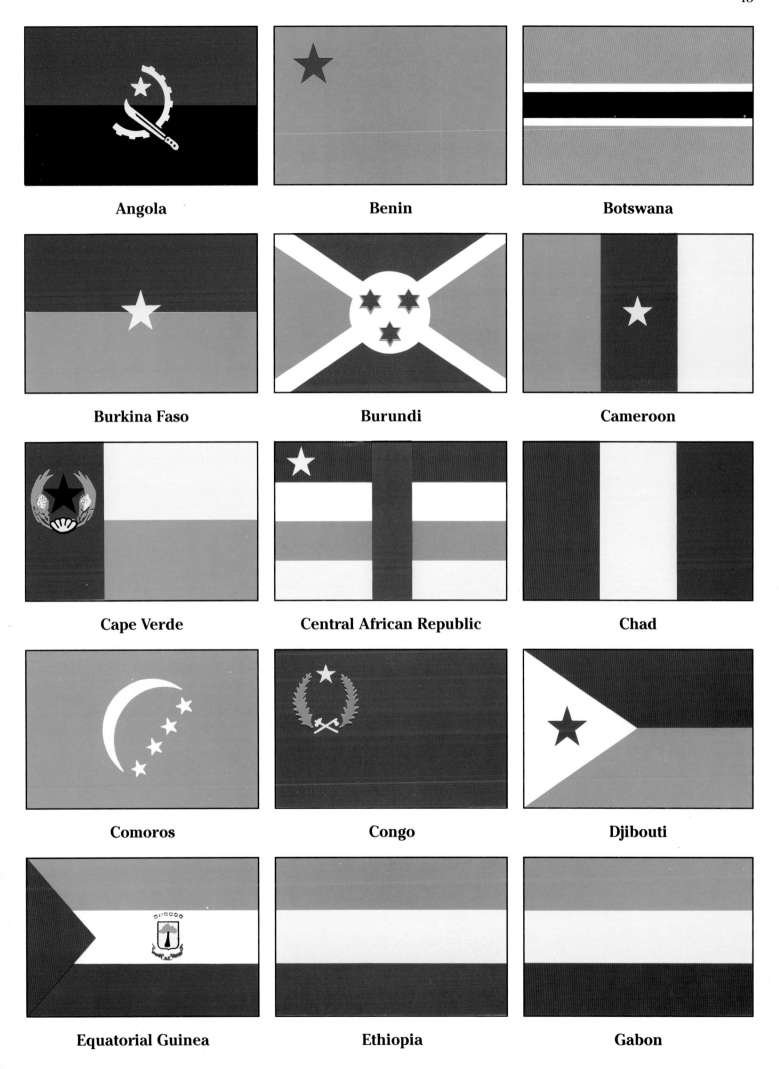

Angola

Benin

Botswana

Burkina Faso

Burundi

Cameroon

Cape Verde

Central African Republic

Chad

Comoros

Congo

Djibouti

Equatorial Guinea

Ethiopia

Gabon

Once a French colony and now an Islamic republic, **Comoros** (formerly Comoro Islands) adopted its present flag after the 1978 coup. The flag uses the traditional Islamic crescent, and four stars to represent the four main islands.

The **Congo** adopted a pan-African tricolor when it became independent from France in 1960, but changed to a Communist-style red banner when a Socialist government came into power in 1969. Compare the flag of the Congo to that of Zaire, the former Belgian Congo.

The former French colony of **Djibouti** became independent on 27 June 1977, adopting a flag that features the red, white and blue of the colonial flag with the green of the pan-African palette.

Adopted on 12 October 1968, the colors of the flag of **Equatorial Guinea** include a mixture of the French and pan-African colors.

The present flag of **Ethiopia**, a horizontal tricolor of pan-African green, yellow and red, green at the top and red at the bottom, existed prior to 1894, when it took the form of three pennants of the same colors, one above the other. In 1898, the first Ethiopian (then Abyssinian) mission which visited France hoisted these colors as a flag.

The colors represent the three traditional parts of Ethiopia: Tiger is red, Choa is green and Amhara is yellow. They also also can be seen to symbolize the Christian trinity: Father (yellow), Son (red) and Holy Ghost (green). Or they may possibly represent the three Christian virtues of faith (red), hope (green) and charity (yellow).

An ancient monarchy, Ethiopia's form of government remained largely the same until 1975, when the monarchy—overthrown in 1974—was abolished and replaced by a Socialist republic.

The green stripe on the **Gabon** flag represents the nation's lumber industry, the blue notes that it is a maritime nation

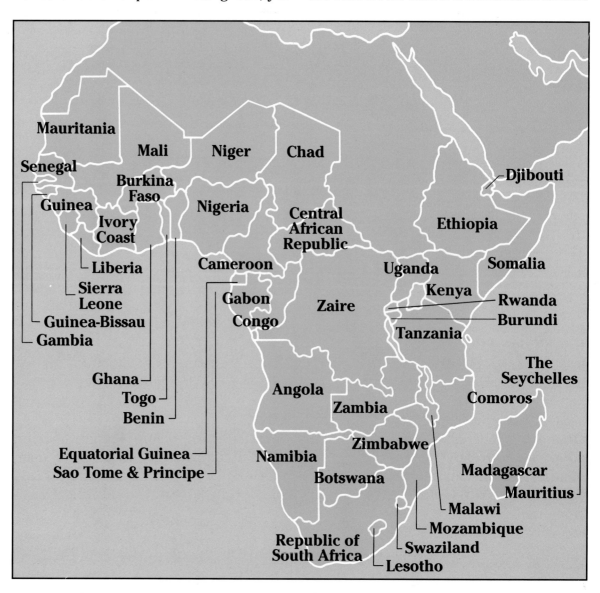

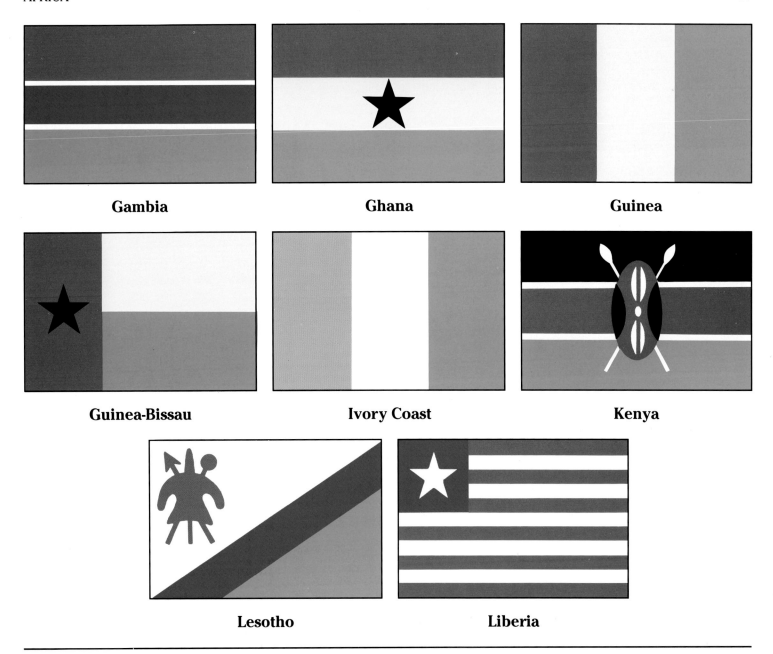

Gambia

Ghana

Guinea

Guinea-Bissau

Ivory Coast

Kenya

Lesotho

Liberia

and the gold is a reference to the fact that the equator runs through the country. These colors were officially adopted on 9 August 1960.

As in the flag of Gabon, the green in the flag of **Gambia** is a reference to natural resources, while the blue represents the Gambia River. The white is a reference to national unity and the red a reference to the sun. Gambia adopted this flag on 18 February 1967.

Adopted on 6 March 1957, the flag of **Ghana** was the first modern state to adopt what are now known as the pan-African colors. This flag was based on that of Ethiopia, the oldest independent state in modern Africa. The black star represents African freedom. The flag has been in use continuously except for a brief period in 1964-1966.

Officially first flown on 10 November 1958, the flag of **Guinea** is a horizontal tricolor based directly on the French tricolor, but incorporating pan-African colors then in use in Ethiopia and Ghana.

Though the design dates to 1961, the flag of **Guinea-Bissau** was officially adopted on 24 September 1973. The black star of the African Party for the Independence of Guinea-Bissau is superimposed on the pan-African colors.

The design for the flag of the **Ivory Coast** is based on the French tricolor, with the colors based on the flag of Niger, another former French colony. Officially adopted on 3 December 1959, the orange represents the northern plains and the green the southern forests. The white stands for unity, but could also be said to represent ivory.

The colors of the **Kenya** flag are based on those of the Kenya African National Union (KANU) which led the move toward independence. The color black represents the people, red their blood and green their national resources. The white represents unity. Adopted on 12 December 1963, the flag also includes the traditional shield of the Masai tribe.

The most prominent feature of the **Lesotho** flag is the shield with crossed spear and war club that suggests the people's readiness to defend the nation. Officially adopted in 1966, the colors symbolize the land (green), peace (white) and the sky and its precious rain (blue). These colors, plus red, were used in the 1966 flag.

**Liberia** was founded in 1821 by the American Colonization Society as an experiment in the colonization of Africa by African-Americans. The Society bought land and resettled freed slaves from America. In 1847, the colony became an independent republic, and in 1857 it absorbed African Maryland, which had also been started as a colony in 1821, and became a republic in a similar way. Adopted on 26 July 1847, the Liberian flag is based on an earlier flag, and consists of 11 equal horizontal stripes, six red and five white, on a blue canton with a white five-pointed star.

The flag of the **Malagasy Republic** (Madagascar) dates to those flown by this island nation's Hova Empire in the nineteenth century. Red represents the Volamena family and white the Volafotsi family. The green was added to denote the fertile lowlands. In its present form, the flag was adopted on 21 October 1958.

The flag of **Malawi** was first adopted by the Malawi Congress party in 1953 and first flown over an independent Malawi on 6 July 1964. The black represents the people, red the blood spilled by patriots and green suggests the country's natural resources.

As had been the case with Guinea, the flag of **Mali** was a tricolor based on the design of the French flag, but utilizing the pan-African color scheme. It was first flown on 1 March 1961.

An Islamic republic, **Mauritania** chose the Islamic crescent but also uses two of the pan-African colors in deference to a sizable African population. The flag was first flown on 1 April 1959.

The colors of the flag of **Mauritius** symbolize (from the top) the red blood shed by patriots, the blue of the Indian Ocean in which the island nation lies, the golden light of independence and, of course, the green fertility of the land. The flag was officially adopted on 12 March 1968.

First flown over an independent nation on 5 September 1974, the flag of **Mozambique** was derived from that of the Front for the Liberation of Mozambique (FRELIMO). The colors are pan-African, and the star represents internationalism.

Until the time of independence on 21 March 1990, **Namibia** saw many flags flown over its territory. Seized from Germany by South Africa in 1915, it remained as the League of Nations (later the United Nations) mandate of Southwest Africa until 1970, when the United Nations withdrew the mandate. South Africa refused to relinquish the territory, and battled local Marxist rebels and Cuban troops for 20 years before Namibia became independent. The present flag is based on that of the pre-independence Southwest African Peoples Organization (SWAPO).

Officially adopted on 23 November 1959, the flag of **Niger** uses green to represent hope, as well as fertility, and orange to represent the northern plains, as well as the omnipresent equatorial sun. Nearby Ivory Coast chose identical colors, based on similar symbolism, for its flag.

Officially adopted on 1 October 1960, the flag of **Nigeria** is a classic tricolor with the green representing natural resources and agriculture, and the white denoting unity. Ironically, an almost identical tricolor was used by the white African government of Rhodesia between 1968 and 1979 until that nation became Zimbabwe. Between 1976 and 1970, the Nigerian region of Biafra was independent under a flag similar to that of Malawi.

Adopted in September 1961, the flag of **Rwanda** is a simple tricolor in the pan-

African scheme that is identical to that of Guinea, but with the addition of the black letter *R*. The letter—which stands not only for Rwanda, but for 'referendum, republic and revolution'—was added to differentiate the flag from Guinea's, although the nations are on opposite sides of Africa.

**Sao Tome & Principe**, once a Portuguese colony, became independent on 12 July 1975. The pan-African colors of the flag are complemented by two stars representing this tiny island nation's two main islands.

A former French colony, **Senegal** became independent in 1959 as part of the Mali Confederation, but broke away in June 1960. The flag, adopted in September 1960, is identical to that of Mali, except for the green star.

The **Seychelles** are an island republic off the coast of east Africa which became independent in 1976. The colors are those of the two leading political parties, but they also symbolize the struggle of the people (red) and the rich agricultural resources (green). The white waves symbolize unity and the Indian Ocean.

The flag of **Sierra Leone** was officially adopted on 27 April 1961. The colors represent the deep harbor at Freetown (blue), the mountains of the interior (green) and unity (white).

Long divided among the British, French and Italian colonies, the Somali people formed an independent **Somalia** on 26 June 1960 and continue to fight to liberate portions of traditional Somali land located in the Ogaden region of

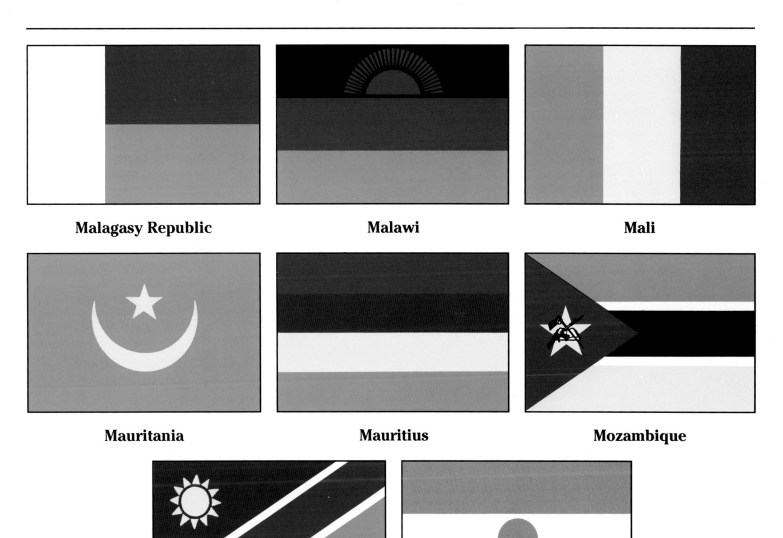

**Malagasy Republic**　　　**Malawi**　　　**Mali**

**Mauritania**　　　**Mauritius**　　　**Mozambique**

**Namibia**　　　**Niger**

Ethiopia. The flag is based on the color of the United Nations flag, with the star representing African freedom.

The present flag of the **Republic of South Africa** dates back to the Union Nationality and Flag Act of 1927, which stated that the national flag of what was then known as the *Union* of South Africa should be: 'Three horizontal stripes of equal width from top to bottom, orange, white and blue, and in the center of the white stripe the old Orange Free State flag hanging vertically spread in full, with the Union Jack adjoining horizontally spread in full towards the pole, and the old Transvaal Vierkleur adjoining equidistant from the margin of the white stripe. The flags shall all be of the same size and their shape shall be proportionally the same as the National Flag, and the width of each equal to one third of the width of the white stripe.'

The Orange Free State flag was placed so that the red, white and blue inset would be on the side nearest to the Union Jack. The small flags were placed centrally in the white stripe of the whole flag. From 31 May 1928, when the flag was first hoisted, until 1961, when South Africa became a republic, whenever the British Union Jack was hoisted, the South African flag was flown as well. Today it is the sole flag of the republic.

The flag of **Swaziland** is based on the 1941 banner of the Emasotsha Regiment of the Swazi Pioneer Corps that served with the British Army during World War II. The flag was adopted on 30 October 1967, nearly a year before Swaziland's independence.

Adopted on 30 June 1964, the flag of **Tanzania** is based on the pre-independence banner of the Tanganyika African National Union (TANU). The TANU flag was green and black, but blue (symbolizing the Indian Ocean) was added when the former British island colony of Zanzibar joined Tanganyika to form the United Republic of Tanzania. The pre-independence Afro-Shirazi party in Zanzibar had a flag of blue, black and green.

The stripes of the flag of **Togo** represent faith and hope, as well as natural resources and the moral basis of the nation. The red is seen as representative of charity, fidelity and love. These colors are, of course, also the pan-African colors. The white star denotes purity. The flag was officially adopted on 27 April 1960.

Adopted on 9 October 1962, the flag of **Uganda** was based on that of the ruling Uganda People's Congress. The black represents the people, the yellow represents the sun and red represents 'universal fraternity.' The crane at the center was a clever device chosen because it had *never* been a symbol of any group in Uganda and was hence neutral.

Prior to independence in 1960, **Zaire** was the Belgian Congo. At that time, its flag was light blue with a golden, five-pointed star. On ceremonial occasions, however, the Belgian tricolor was always flown. The present flag was adopted in November 1971. It features the pan-African color scheme, as well as the symbol of the Popular Movement of the Revolution (MPR), the party of president Mobutu, who declared Zaire to be a single party state in 1971.

The four colors of the flag of **Zambia** were originally used by the United Nationalist Independence Party (UNIP) and were adopted in the present form on 24 October 1964. The orange, as well as the green, symbolize the country's natural resource, while black stands for the people and red for the blood shed in the quest for independence. The eagle indicates Zambia's ability to rise above adversity.

**Zimbabwe** was a highly developed nation in ancient Africa whose culture remained legendary even after the nation disappeared. The British colonized the region as Rhodesia, naming it for the explorer Cecil Rhodes. The white government of Rhodesia declared independence in 1965 and adopted a green, white and green tricolor (like Nigeria's) in 1968. The government was taken over by the black majority on 18 April 1980 and the country's name was changed to Zimbabwe. The bird on the present flag was based on a soapstone carving found in the ruins of ancient Zimbabwe and had also been used on the center panel of the Rhodesian tricolor.

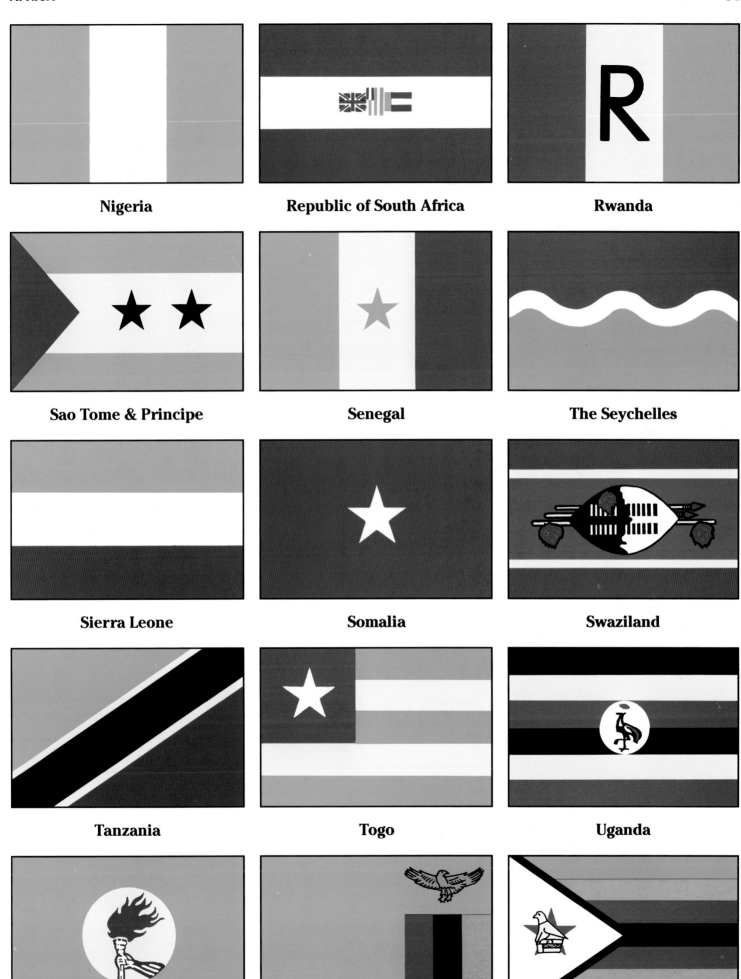

**Nigeria**

**Republic of South Africa**

**Rwanda**

**Sao Tome & Principe**

**Senegal**

**The Seychelles**

**Sierra Leone**

**Somalia**

**Swaziland**

**Tanzania**

**Togo**

**Uganda**

**Zaire**

**Zambia**

**Zimbabwe**

# ASIA

Prior to the reign of King Amanullah (1919-1929), the national flag of **Afghanistan** was black and bore a device with a mosque within a wreath in white. In 1929, he altered the flag to a vertical tricolor of black, red and green. The black is said to represent the blot upon the country before she gained her independence. The red is the sacrifice made in obtaining this independence, and the green stands for both Islam and the progress made since gaining independence. In Amanullah's time, and during the first years of the reign of Nadir Khan, a white emblem consisting of an eight-pointed star enclosing a device of a mosque and crossed swords was placed in the center of the red portion. When the monarchy was overthrown in 1973, the flag became a horizontal tricolor composed of the same colors, with a small, rising sun in the canton corner.

The East Bengal component of British India, and officially part of Pakistan after 1947, **Bangladesh** (Bengal Nation) became independent in 1971. Adopted on 25 January 1972, the flag was designed by Serajul Alam, whose name means 'light of the flag.' The green symbolizes the lush vegetation of Bangladesh, while the red disk represents the blood shed in the battle for independence. A yellow outline map of the country was originally included but was deleted in 1972.

The colors of the flag of **Bhutan** represent the temporal authority of the king (yellow) and the spiritual authority of Buddhism (orange). The dragon refers to Bhutan's reputation as the 'Land of the Dragon,' which derives from the ancient belief that thunder was the voice of dragons living in Bhutan's mountain valleys. The origin of the flag is uncertain but it probably predates the nineteenth century.

The Sultanate of **Brunei** dates to the sixteenth century, at which time it had a solid yellow flag. Remaining under British 'protection' from 1888, it emerged in 1984 as Brunei Darussalam. The flag was adopted in 1959 when Brunei became self-governing.

Known alternately as **Cambodia** and **Kampuchea**, this former French Southeast Asian colony has known almost constant suffering and turmoil since the 1960s. During this time, numerous flags have flown over the region. All of them have, however, been generally similar to the present flag with the ancient temple of Angkor Wat superimposed on a red and blue background. The 1948 to 1970, the royal flag was a horizontal tricolor of blue, red and blue, with Angkor Wat in the center.

In the old imperial days, the flag of **China** was yellow with one dominant feature on it—the dragon. The dragon on the Emperor's standard had five claws on each foot, and it was said that by a standing law of the Empire, no mandarin or nobleman, on pain of death, should show more than four claws on each foot of the dragon upon his flags. Adopted in 1912, the first republican flag had five equal horizontal stripes (*from top*): red, yellow, blue, white and black; one for each of China's four regions, with the fifth representing the country's Islamic citizens. In 1928, the republic adopted a flag that incorporated the sun of the Kuomintang (Nationalist) party. Plain red with a dark blue canton with the

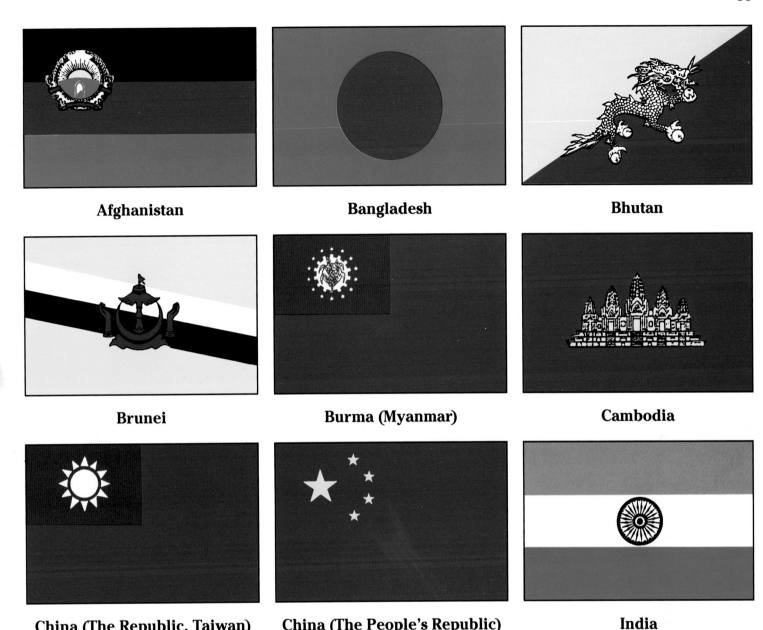

**Afghanistan**

**Bangladesh**

**Bhutan**

**Brunei**

**Burma (Myanmar)**

**Cambodia**

**China (The Republic, Taiwan)**

**China (The People's Republic)**

**India**

Kuomintang's 12-rayed star in white, this flag survives today as the flag of the Nationalist government of the **Republic of China**, which has been in exile on the island of Taiwan since 1949.

When the Communists under Mao Tse-tung (Mao Zedong) took control of the mainland of China in 1949, the **People's Republic of China** was established. This included adoption of the present, mostly red, flag of China, which was modeled after the flag of the USSR. The large star represents communism, and the smaller ones represent the four classes of society: peasants, workers, bourgeoisie and merchants.

Prior to gaining its independence in 1947, **India** flew the Union Jack of Britain, with the Star of India surmounted by the Imperial Crown in the center. This design

had the rays of the star shown in the margin. The current flag, adopted on 22 July 1947, is a horizontal tricolor, with orange representing courage and sacrifice, green representing faith and chivalry, and white representing truth and peace. The wheel is the *dharma chakra*, a spinning wheel representing the 'wheel of life.' This wheel was adopted by Mohandas Ghandi in 1931 as the symbol of his All India Congress Committee (later Congress Party). It is intended to represent humility and self reliance.

The red and white flag of **Indonesia** dates to 1293 and was the flag used by Prince Jayakatong in his revolt against the kingdom of Singasari. Adopted as the flag of the Majapahit Empire, the flag was revived in 1922 by students demanding independence from the Netherlands and in 1928 by the Indonesia Nationals Party. The flag first flew over an independent Indonesia on 27 December 1949.

**Japan** is the land of the rising sun, and the flag adopted in 1870 contains a representation of the sun as a plain red ball on a white field. If rays are added to the plain ball of the sun, the inner two-thirds of the flag put forth 16 rays to the edges of the flag, five to the top, five to the bottom and three to each of the sides. During World War II, this configuration was the imperial battle flag. Prior to and during World War II, the flags of the naval officers showed the sun with eight rays, three to the top, three to the bottom and one to each side. The Japanese Royal Standard is red, charged with the state 'Mon' of Japan (Kiku-non-hana-mon), a conventional golden chrysanthemum of 16 rays. The standard of the empress is similar, but swallow-tailed. That of the prince imperial is the same as that flown by the emperor but it has the addition of a narrow white outline in the shape of a frame placed round the chrysanthemum. The other imperial princes and princesses have their chrysanthemum on a white ground, the standard having a broad red border.

Traditionally known as **Burma**, **Myanmar** became independent of Britain in 1948, but it did not adopt the present flag until 3 January 1974. The red is symbolic of courage and tenacity, and the white stars originated during the struggle to liberate the country from the Japanese during World War II and represent the country's seven states and seven provinces.

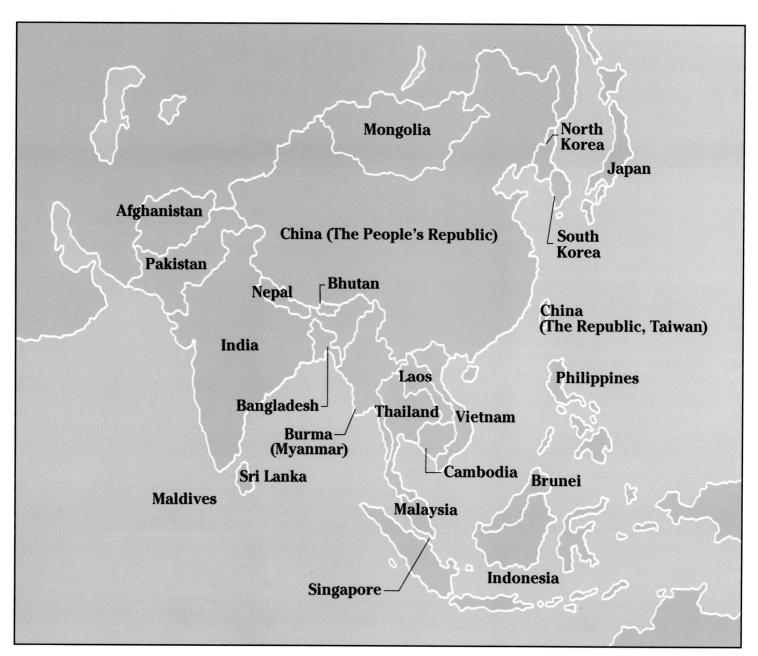

The flag of **South Korea** (Republic of Korea), the *pakwa* or *taeguk*, carries the yin-yang symbol which represents any two opposite and yet relative elements in nature, such as male and female, earth and sky or water and earth. Both are within the circle, and so curved and interlocked that they are equal in area. The four kwae (hexagrams) in the corners represent the cardinal directions; the seasons; and the sun, moon, earth and heaven. The flag was first flown in August 1882 and officially adopted on 27 January 1883. It was readopted by the Republic of Korea in 1948 after the end of foreign occupation by the Japanese (1910-1945) and the Allies (1945-1948).

The flag of **North Korea** (Korean Democratic People's Republic) was adopted officially on 8 September 1948. The blue is seen as representative of peace, while the red signifies socialism. The star is said to be based on the traditional Korean *taeguk*, or symbol of the universe.

The flag of **Laos** was adopted when the People's Democratic Republic was declared on 3 December 1975. The colors are reminiscent of those of neighboring Vietnam. The 1947-1975 flag of the former kingdom of Laos was red with a trio of elephants under a white parasol, a reference to Laos as the 'land of a million elephants.'

Adopted on 16 September 1963 at the time of independence from Britain, the flag of **Malaysia** bears 14 stripes, one for each Malay state. During the 1950-1963 period when it was the British possession of **Malaya**, there were 10 stripes, and between 1965 and 1974, there were 13. Singapore became independent, but a federal district for the capital (Kuala Lumpur) was added nine years later. The star and crescent are symbolic of Islam.

The **Maldives** are an island republic off the southwest coast of India that became independent of Britain in 1965. The red is the color of the old Arab trading flags, while the green and the crescent are symbolic of Islam.

The basic form of the flag of **Mongolia** dates to 1924 and the proclamation of the Mongolian People's Republic, but

*Above:* Japan's flag, with its distinctive rising sun symbol, features prominently in this New Year's celebration.

the present flag was adopted on 23 February 1949. Sky blue has been the national color for centuries and red is symbolic of socialism. The latter has been retained despite the demise of Mongolia's experiment with communism.

**Nepal** is the only country in the world without a rectangular national flag. The shape is seen as symbolic of the peaks of the Himalayas and red is the national color. Prior to the twentieth century, two pennants were flown together, with the sun and moon representing the two ruling families. Since the demise of these two families in 1951, the sun and moon are expressive of the hope that Nepal will endure as long as the celestial bodies.

Officially adopted on 14 August 1947, the flag of **Pakistan** actually dates back to the green flag of the Muslim League and the flag first raised by Islamic nationalists in 1906. The color green, as well as the star and crescent, are Islamic symbols, and the white refers to the religious minorities living within the country.

The **Philippines** flag was first raised officially on 12 June 1898 at the end of the Spanish colonial period. The United States, which took control of the country later that year, frowned on the flag and banned its use from 1907 to 1921. So too did the Japanese who occupied the Philippines between 1941 and 1945. By a 1936 agreement, the United States granted complete independence to the Philippines in 1946, but had actually recognized the flag as official on 14 October 1943. The eight rays on the sun refer to the Philippines' eight original provinces.

The flag of **Singapore** was first flown on 3 December 1959 when it became an autonomous colony within the British Commonwealth. Between 1963 and 1965, while Singapore was a province of Malaysia, the flag flew as a Malaysian provincial flag. It was first raised as a *national* flag on 9 August 1965. The five stars stand for democracy, equality, justice, peace and progress. The crescent is symbolic of Islam.

The flag of **Sri Lanka** (formerly the British colony of **Ceylon**) was adopted on 22 May 1972. The portion containing the lion is a replica of the banner of the last king of Ceylon, who was deposed by the British in 1815. This flag was re-adopted in 1948. Added in 1972, the green represents the Hindu (Tamil) people and the orange stands for the Islamic (Moor) minorities.

The national flag of **Thailand** (formerly **Siam**) was originally plain red, but in December 1899 this was changed to red with a white elephant in the center. The legend of the white elephant begins before Zacca, the legendary founder of the nation, was born, when Zacca's mother dreamt that she brought forth a white elephant. Zacca, after a metamorphosis of 80,000 changes, concluded his extremely varied experiences as a white elephant, and therefore was received into the company of the gods. The white elephant thus stands in the same relation to Thailand as a patron saint would in Christianity. In November 1916, the flag was changed to a horizontal pattern of red with two white stripes, each of the latter being one-sixth the depth of the flag and being placed one-sixth of the depth from the top and bottom of the flag respectively. A year later, King Rama VI decided to introduce blue into the design (blue being the color of the navy flags and also having been used in the ancient service flags of Thailand), and so the broad central stripe of red was changed to blue. He also ordered the elephant removed so that if the flag was flown upside down, it would be the same. Thus, the present national flag, known as the 'Trairanga Flag,' was adopted officially on 28 September 1917.

**Vietnam** became independent of France in 1954 as two nations: the **Democratic Republic of Vietnam** (North Vietnam) and the **Republic of Vietnam** (South Vietnam). North Vietnam forcibly united the country by its conquest of South Vietnam on 30 April 1975 and the flag of North Vietnam became the flag of the entire nation. This flag was adopted on 29 September 1945 by Ho Chi Minh's Nationalists, although the basic design dates to 1940. The flag of South Vietnam in the 1954-1975 period was overall yellow with three horizontal red stripes across the center.

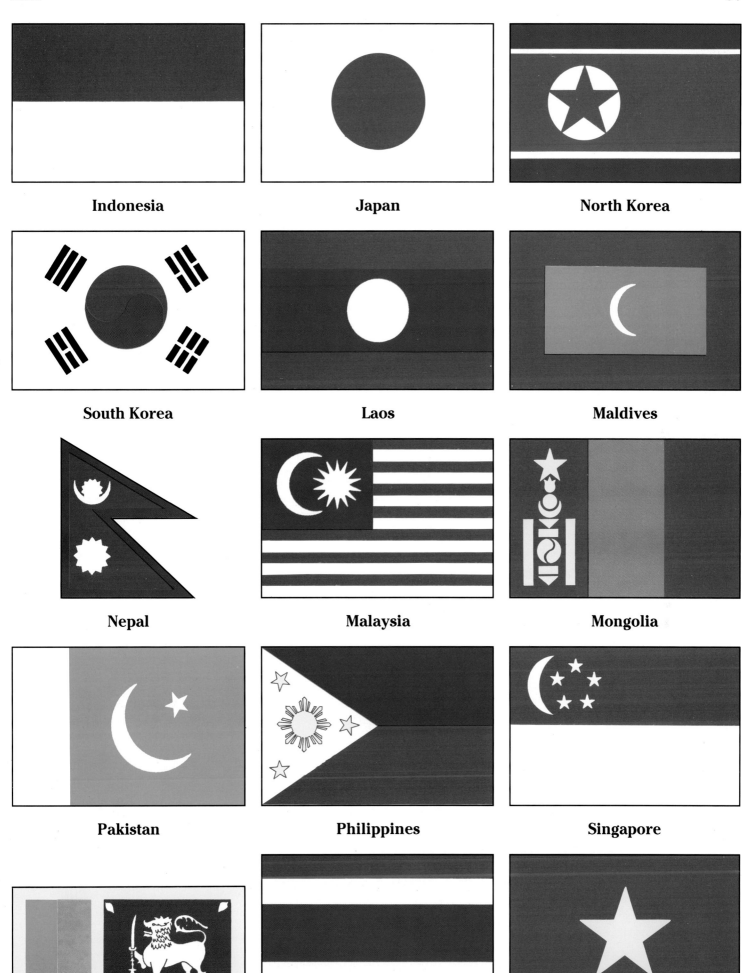

Indonesia

Japan

North Korea

South Korea

Laos

Maldives

Nepal

Malaysia

Mongolia

Pakistan

Philippines

Singapore

Sri Lanka

Thailand

Vietnam

# OCEANIA

The flag of **Australia** was first flown on 16 September 1901 and officially adopted on 22 May 1909. It has a large seven-pointed star beneath the Union Jack and the constellation known as the Southern Cross represented by four smaller seven-pointed stars and a still smaller five-pointed star. The points on the star stand for each of the six states plus the Northern Territory. This Southern Cross constellation, which is not visible in the Northern Hemisphere, is an important symbol for people south of the equator and is also used by New Zealand and Papau New Guinea. The constellation was first used on a flag by miners who stood against a corrupt police force in the Eureka Stockade incident in Australia in 1854.

Even Alexander Humboldt, who sailed with Captain James Cook on his second voyage, felt the influence. 'We saw distinctly,' he wrote, 'for the first time, the Cross of the South on the night of the fourth and fifth of July, in the sixteenth degree of latitude. It was strongly inclined and appeared from time to time between the clouds, the center of which, furrowed by uncondensed lightnings, reflected a silver light. The pleasure felt on discovering the Southern Cross was warmly shared by such of the crew as had lived in the colonies. In the solitude of the seas we hail a star as a friend, from whom we have been long separated. Among the Portuguese and the Spaniards, peculiar motives seem to increase this feeling. A religious sentiment attaches them to a constellation, the form of which recalls the sign of the faith planted by their ancestors in the deserts of the New World.'

*Right:* **The aircraft of the Roulettes, the official aerobatic team of the Royal Australian Air Force, have the flag of Australia prominently displayed on their fuselages.**

**Australia**

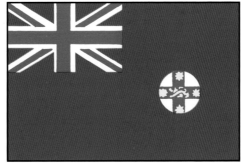

**New South Wales**

**Queensland**

**South Australia**

**Tasmania**

**Victoria**

**Western Australia**

**Northern Territory**

**Norfolk Island**

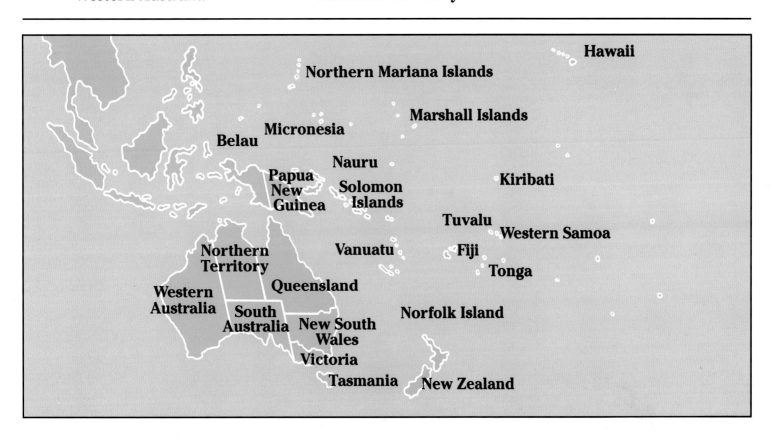

Also known as the Republic of **Palau**, **Belau** is a group of Pacific Islands that was under United States administration as United Nations Trust Territory until 1986. The yellow disc represents the moon. Blue represents neither sky nor sea but rather independence.

The flag of **Fiji**—with the British Union Jack in the canton—was officially adopted on 10 October 1970 at the time of independence. However, it is essentially identical to the flag flown by Fiji for almost a century as a member of the British Empire. The coat-of-arms with the Cross of St George, combined with palm trees and bananas, dates to 1871.

Formerly the Gilbert Islands, a British protectorate, **Kiribati** achieved independence in 1979 and adopted a flag which features the frigate bird coat-of-arms which dates from 1937. The overall design of the flag was chosen in a national contest.

Like Belau, the Republic of the **Marshall Islands** became self-governing in 1979 and formed a free association with the United States in 1986. The flag dates from 1979 and features blue for the Pacific Ocean and orange for courage and prosperity. The rays of the star represent the 20 island municipalities and four administrative districts.

The Federated States of **Micronesia** are part of the United Nations Trust Territory administered by the United States until 1985. The color is based on the United Nations flag, with the stars representing the four major island states of Kosrae, Pohnpei (the capital), Truk and Yap.

Until 1968, **Nauru** was a joint trusteeship of Australia, New Zealand and the United Kingdom. The star represents Nauru itself and its position in the Pacific Ocean relative to the equator.

Officially adopted on 12 June 1902, the flag of **New Zealand**, like Australia's, bears the Southern Cross, although it contains four—not five—five-pointed stars, one above, one beneath and one on each side, all in red rather than white, as in the Australian flag.

The upper and lower stars serve to indicate the position of the South Pole as

Dubhe and Merak in the Great Bear do that of the North Pole. Just as the Big Dipper never sets in the Northern Hemisphere, so does the Southern Cross never set in Australia or New Zealand.

The Commonwealth of the **Northern Mariana Islands** was an American-administered Trust Territory until 1976 when the islands became an American Commonwealth. The blue represents the Pacific Ocean. The star is superimposed upon a taga stone, a relic of the islanders' Chamorro ancestors.

Like the flags of Australia and New Zealand, the flag of **Papua New Guinea** carries the Southern Cross. The yellow bird of paradise represents the national bird. The flag first flew over a nation independent of Australia's trusteeship on 16 September 1975, although it dates from 1971.

Having become independent of Britain on 7 July 1978, the **Solomon Islands** adopted a flag whose colors symbolize the rich green of the land and the blue of the sea and sky. The stars are representative of the five major islands.

The Pacific island kingdom of **Tonga** first adopted its flag on 4 November 1875. Designed by Prince Uelingatoni, Ngu Tupoumalohi and Reverend Shirley Baker, the flag represented the wish of King George Tupou that the flag 'have the cross of Jesus … and be red in color to represent the blood shed on the cross for our salvation.'

The Republic of **Vanuatu** achieved independence in 1980. The yellow lines roughly trace the shape of the archipelago of islands that form the nation. The circular device represents a boar's tusk.

Officially adopted on 24 February 1949, the flag of **Western Samoa** was designed by their highnesses Tupua Tamasese Mea'ole and Malietoa Tanumafili II, and incorporates the Southern Cross. Western Samoa remained a mandate of New Zealand until 1962, during which time the flag was always flown along with that of New Zealand over ships at sea. The colors are representative of courage (red), purity (white) and freedom (blue).

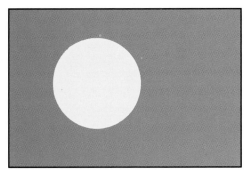

**Belau**

**Fiji**

**Kiribati**

**Marshall Islands**

**Micronesia**

**Nauru**

**New Zealand**

**Northern Mariana Islands**

**Papua New Guinea**

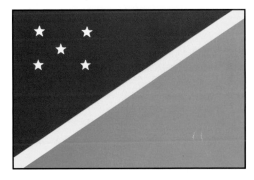

**Solomon Islands**

**Tonga**

**Tuvalu**

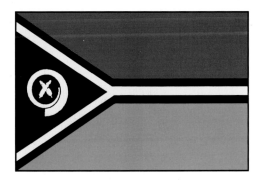

**Vanuatu**

**Western Samoa**

# SOUTH AMERICA

Officially adopted on 25 July 1816 at the time of independence, the national flag of **Argentina** is a horizontal tricolor. Traditionally, a sun is placed in the white stripe, although the flag appears both ways. The sun represents the *Sol de Mayo*, which is the sun that shown through clouds on 25 May 1810 as the people began to agitate against Spanish rule.

**Bolivia**, formerly Upper Peru, took its name from the great liberator Simon Bolivar in 1825. The present flag, a horizontal tricolor of red, yellow and green, red at the top and green at the bottom, was officially adopted on 14 July 1888. Red signifies courage, yellow signifies gold and green stands for agricultural resources.

The Spanish flag was hoisted by Pinzon at Cape St Augustine in January 1500, and the Portuguese arrived at Porto Seguro the following April. 'Terra da Vera Cruz,' as it was then named, was the real beginning of **Brazil**. The Spanish flags were the red stripes on the yellow in the old form. Those of the Portuguese were the white shield with five blue shields bordered with red and castles thereon, with the five black balls on blue, also bordered with red. After Portugal was conquered by Spain, the Dutch arrived at Bahia and hoisted their tricolor, which remained for 20 years at different places along the coast until Portugal, once again emancipated from Spain, resumed possession of its American colonies. In 1808 these colonies became a refuge for the Portuguese king, whose eldest son threw off the parental yoke in 1822. Brazil then became an empire with a flag of its own, which in 1889 was replaced by that of the republic. During its imperial days, Brazil's flag was green with a yellow diamond—as now—and a shield flanked with sprigs of coffee and tobacco. Crown, shield and sprigs have disappeared, and in their place is a blue celestial globe, adopted on 15 November 1889, with a white equator on which is inscribed in green 'Ordem e Progresso' (order and progress). The stars shown are those which were in the sky at the time of independence.

**Chile** was under the Spanish flag until 1810, when it regained its independence under Bernardo O'Higgins, the son of one of the Viceroys of Peru. The colors are based on those worn by the Indians in the national epic *La Aravcana*. After independence, many different tricolors—with and without stars—were used until this one was officially adopted in October 1817. It is said to have been designed by an American mercenary named Charles Wood and to be based on a greatly simplified version of the American flag.

The Republic of **Colombia**, in the north of South America, was formerly known as New Granada, and was freed from Spain in 1819 by Simon Bolivar. Its

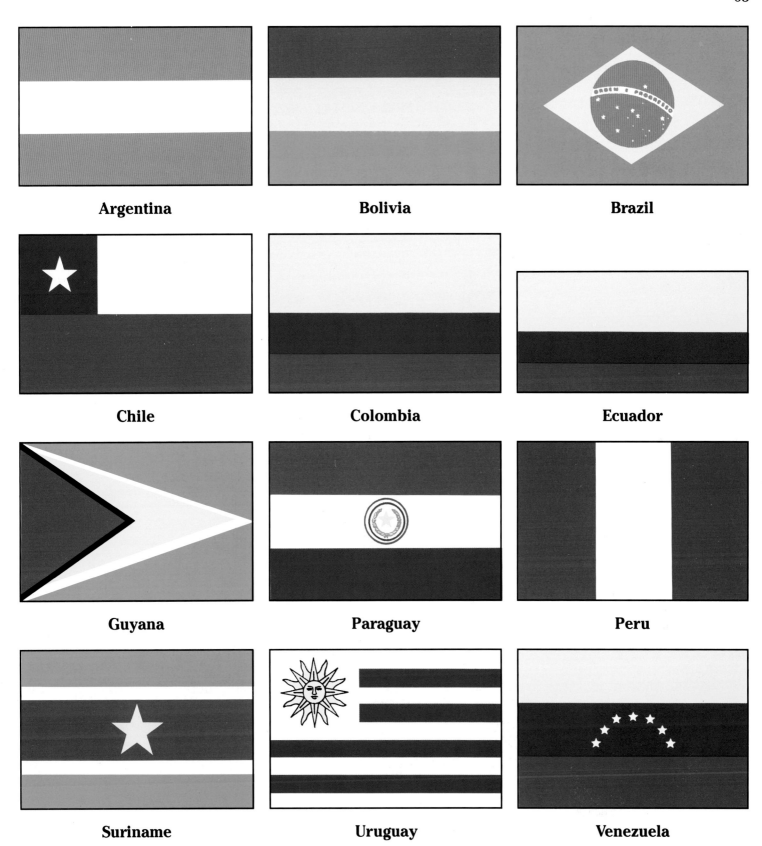

**Argentina**

**Bolivia**

**Brazil**

**Chile**

**Colombia**

**Ecuador**

**Guyana**

**Paraguay**

**Peru**

**Suriname**

**Uruguay**

**Venezuela**

national flag is a simple tricolor, with the gold symbolic of the mineral gold of the region, the blue for the Atlantic Ocean and the red is a reference to Spain. The colors date to the early nineteenth century, but this flag was officially adopted on 26 November 1861. A similar flag is used by Ecuador and Venezuela.

The flag of **Ecuador** closely resembles that of Colombia, its northern neighbor, but its blue stripe is lighter. The coat-of-arms consists of an oval shield containing a landscape that shows a snow-capped mountain rising out of the sea with a steamer thereon and the sun with four of the signs of the Zodiac in the sky. These insignia were adopted upon the Declaration of Independence in 1822. The snow-topped mountain represents the Chimborazo, the highest peak in the country, which is of historic importance during the War of Independence. The steamer stands for commerce, while the four signs in the Zodiac—those of March, April, May and June—mark memorable months in the history of the country. Above the oval is the condor of the Andes, below is a fasces, and on each side are two tricolors. The flag has been in use since 1860, but it was officially adopted on 7 November 1900.

First flown on 26 May 1966, the flag of **Guyana** is known as the 'golden arrowhead,' an artifact seen as symbolic of Guyana's hope for progress in the future. The flag's green background represents the rich forests of this former British colony.

The flag of **Paraguay** is a horizontal tricolor of equal stripes of red at the top, white in the center and blue at the bottom. It is identical to the Netherlands flag, except for the badge on the white stripe. The star represents the Paraguayan *Estrella de Mayo* that shown on 14 May 1821, the night that Paraguay declared independence. The flag was adopted officially on 27 November 1842, but similar flags date back to 1812.

The vertical tricolor of red, white and red was officially adopted on 25 February 1825, but the colors date to 1820 when **Peru** was liberated by Jose de San Martin. The color represents the blood shed in the war of independence, but has also been said to be reminiscent of the color of flamingos.

Formerly Dutch Guyana, **Suriname** became independent of the Netherlands on 25 November 1975, and the predominantly black population chose a flag in the traditional pan-African colors. The gold star expresses the hope for a 'golden future.'

In 1726, the Spaniards established themselves at Montevideo, and until 1828 **Uruguay**—the old *Banda Oriental*—was Spanish and Portuguese by turns. The current national flag of Uruguay was officially adopted on 11 July 1830, although the colors date back to 1812. The design is based on that of the flag of Argentina, which helped in the Uruguayan war of independence. It consists of nine equal horizontal stripes, five white and four light blue, a white canton charged with the *Sol de Mayo* (eight of the rays are straight and eight are wavy).

The horizontal tricolor of **Venezuela** has equal stripes of yellow at the top, blue in the middle and red at the bottom in the center of the blue stripe, with seven, white five-pointed stars arranged in a circle. It was first flown by the leaders of the failed revolution of 1797. On 12 March 1806 it was again hoisted.

The seven stars, one for each original province, date from 1817 and were made permanent in 1859. The flag has, however, remained unchanged since independence in 1830, and subsequently served as the inspiration for the flags of both Ecuador and Colombia.

In the coat-of-arms, the shield is divided into halves horizontally, and the top half is divided in two vertically, the left side being yellow and bearing a sheaf of wheat in white, the right-hand side being red and bearing a tricolor and three sword hilts, while the base is blue and is charged with a white horse. Two horns of plenty form the crest.

*Above:* **The flag of Venezuela flies proudly over the city of Caracas.**

# CENTRAL AMERICA

*Above:* **The countries of Central America are: 1) Belize; 2) Costa Rica; 3) El Salvador; 4) Guatemala; 5) Honduras; 6) Mexico; 7) Nicaragua; and 8) Panama.**

The flag of **Belize** was adopted when British Honduras achieved its independence in 1981. It is based on the flag of the People's United party, which dates from 1950. The dominant symbol in the coat-of-arms is a mahogany tree, which is a reference to the importance of the timber industry.

In 1821, the newly independent former Spanish colonies of Costa Rica, El Salvador, Guatemala and Nicaragua formed the **Central American Federation**. This entity, which survived until 1839, had a horizontal tricolor of blue and white, which was the basis for the individual flags of the five successor states.

The flag of **Costa Rica** consists of five horizontal stripes, blue, red, and white. This flag, in essentially the same form, has been in use since 1848, but it was not officially adopted until 21 October 1964.

Like other former Federation of Central American States countries, **El Salvador** has a simple blue and white tricolor as its national flag. The coat-of-arms consists of a triangular shield, with five conical mountains rising out of the sea, which represent the five volcanoes of the Central American isthmus and the five former nations of the Federation. In the center is a pole upon which is a cap of liberty. The sun's rays appear in the background with the inscription '15 de Septiembre de 1821.' On each side are two of the national flags, and underneath is a scroll bearing the legend 'Dios Union Libertad.' A wreath of laurel tied with

dark blue ribbon encircles the design, while in a circle outside the whole are the words 'Republica de El Salvador en la America Central.'

**Guatemala** flies a vertical tricolor of dark blue, white and dark blue. When the republic was established in 1847, the flag was a horizontal tricolor, the top stripe being half red, half blue, the center stripe white, and the bottom stripe half yellow, half blue. Later it appeared with seven stripes of blue, white, red, yellow, red, white and blue. Its present form came into use around in 1871, although it was adopted officially on 15 September 1968.

Based on the Argentine and Guatemalan flags, the present flag of **Honduras** is a horizontal tricolor of equal stripes of blue, white and blue. In the center of the white stripe are five blue five-pointed stars. The stars are symbolic of the old Central American Federation. The basic form of the flag has been in use since 1866, but it was officially adopted on 18 January 1949.

**Mexico** officially achieved its independence from Spain in September 1821, and the republic was declared in 1823. The tricolor design of the flag was copied from the French flag, but the colors were copied from those of Italy. It has been recorded that the Italians protested at the time, but the Mexicans refused to change their flag. In order to distinguish its flag from that of Mexico, Italy then placed the shield of Savoy in the white stripe in the center. In the center of the

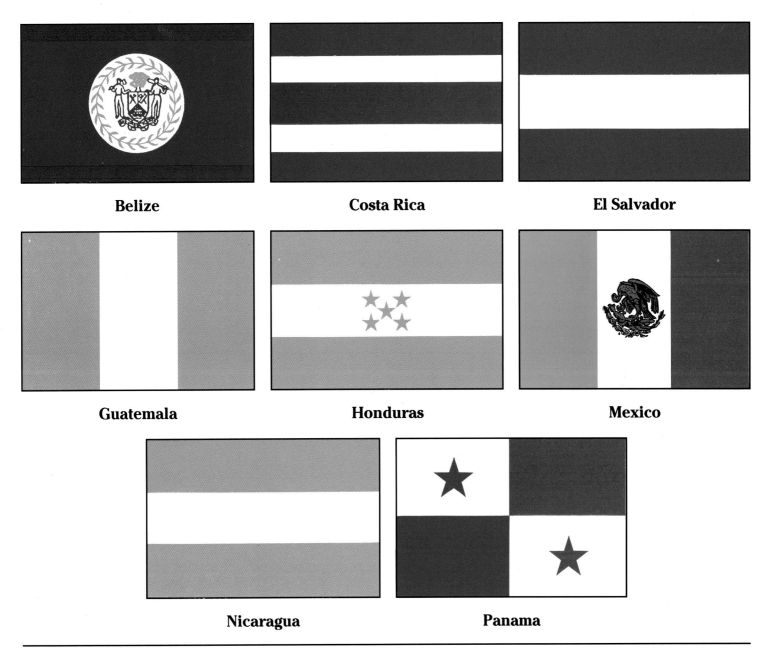

**Belize**

**Costa Rica**

**El Salvador**

**Guatemala**

**Honduras**

**Mexico**

**Nicaragua**

**Panama**

flag is the coat-of-arms of Mexico, an eagle holding a snake in its beak and standing on a prickly pear cactus. A wreath of oak and laurel surrounds the eagle.

Christopher Columbus discovered **Nicaragua** in 1502, and it remained under Spanish rule until 1821 when it joined the Federation of Central American States. When this entity dissolved in 1839, Nicaragua adopted a flag similar to that of its former partners. The national flag is a tricolor with a badge on the white stripe. This badge consists of a triangle, which bears a landscape consisting of five conical mountains rising out of the sea. The design is surrounded by a wreath of oak and laurel, tied with a red bow. Around the top in black lettering is the legend, 'Republica De Nicaragua.' When the leftist Sandinista

party came into power in 1979, their black and red party flag was accorded a status similar to that enjoyed by the Nazi party flag in Germany after 1933. When the Sandinistas were defeated at the polls, their flag lost its special status.

**Panama** became a separate republic in 1903, and the present flag was officially adopted on 4 June 1904. Panama's flag is divided into quarters, the first quarter white, charged with a blue five-pointed star, the second quarter red, the third blue and the fourth quarter white, charged with a red five-pointed star. The colors represent the two ends of the political spectrum from left (red) to right (blue). They also represent the two oceans joined by the Panama Canal. The canal opened in 1914, with a canal zone, under US jurisdiction until 1999, extending five miles on either side.

# THE CARIBBEAN

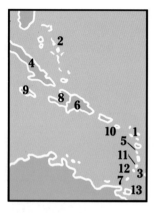

*Above:* **The independent island nations of the Caribbean include: 1) Antigua & Barbuda; 2) The Bahamas; 3) Barbados; 4) Cuba; 5) Dominica; 6) Dominican Republic; 7) Grenada; 8) Haiti; 9) Jamaica; 10) St Kitts & Nevis; 11) St Lucia; 12) St Vincent & The Grenadines; and 13) Trinidad & Tobago.**

The flag of **Antigua & Barbuda** first flew over an independent nation in 1981. The red represents the energy of the people, the black their color and the sun the emergence of the new nation, which is framed in a 'V' for victory.

Officially adopted on 10 July 1973, the flag of **The Bahamas** is predominantly aquamarine, representing the Atlantic Ocean. The gold symbolized the golden sand and the black represents unity.

The trident of Neptune was the symbol of **Barbados** for many years before the flag was officially adopted on 30 November 1966. The blue and gold represent the sea, the sky and the golden beaches.

Columbus discovered **Cuba** when he arrived in the West Indies in 1492, and it remained a Spanish Colony until 1898. In 1902 it was declared an independent republic. The present flag was adopted on 20 May 1902 and was unaffected by Cuba's flirtation with communism.

**Dominica** achieved its independence from Britain on 3 November 1978. The bird on the flag is the sisserou parrot, the indigenous national bird.

The **Dominican Republic** became independent in 1821, only to succumb briefly to Spanish rule between 1861-1863. The present flag was adopted on 6 November 1844 and readopted on 14 September 1863. The colors are those of neighboring Haiti's mid-nineteenth century flag with a cross added to indicate faith.

Officially adopted on 7 February 1974 at the time of independence from Bri-tain, the flag of **Grenada** contains a star for each of the nation's parishes. The symbol on the left celebrates Grenada's role as the world's second largest producer of nutmeg.

**Haiti** was dominated by French buccaneers until it was ceded to France in 1697. Haiti won its independence as the Western Hemisphere's first black republic in 1804, and adopted a flag based on the French tricolor, but with the white (seen as representing white slavers) omitted.

The flag of **Jamaica** was first flown on 6 August 1962. The green symbolizes hope and natural resources, gold also refers to natural wealth, and black indicates past and present hardships.

**St Kitts & Nevis** became independent on 19 September 1983. The two stars are symbolic of the two islands.

The island of **St Lucia** became independent of Britain on 22 February 1979, adopting a predominantly blue flag symbolic of the Caribbean. The triangles are emblematic of two volcano cones, the people and the beaches.

**St Vincent & The Grenadines** became independent of Britain on 27 October 1979. The diamonds represent the three main islands, and a stylized image of the breadfruit, introduced from Tahiti in 1792 by Captain William Bligh.

**Trinidad & Tobago** were two former British possessions united on 31 August 1962. The red of the flag expresses the warmth and the energy of the sun and of the people. Black indicates unity and strength. The design is also reminiscent of the symbol used by SCUBA divers.

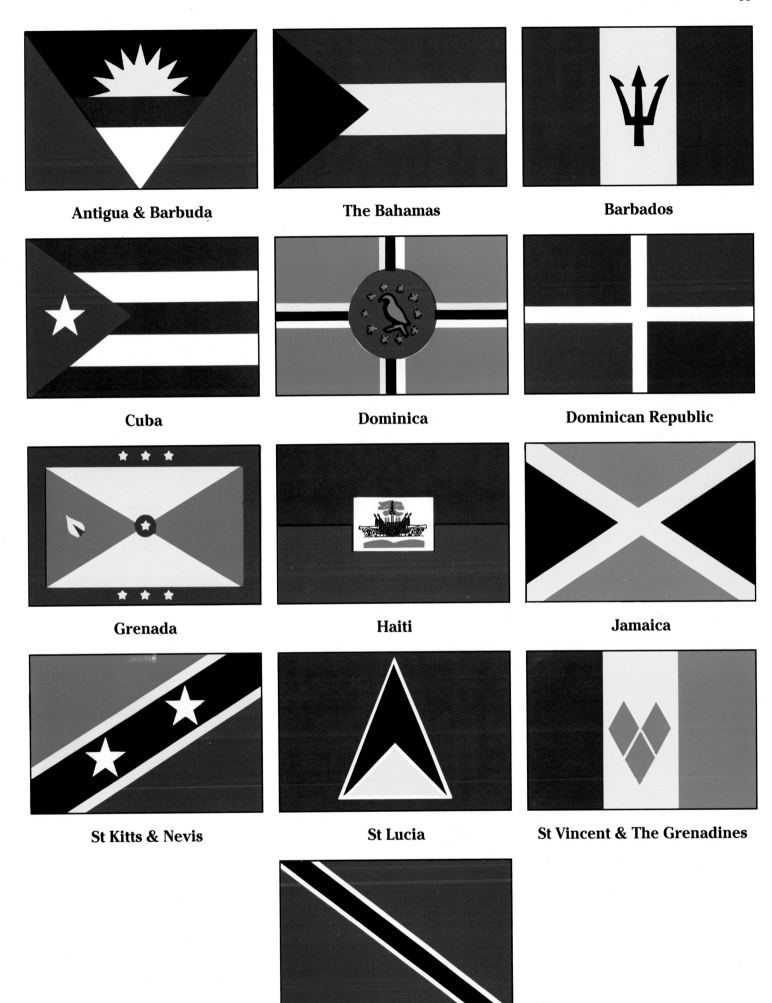

Antigua & Barbuda

The Bahamas

Barbados

Cuba

Dominica

Dominican Republic

Grenada

Haiti

Jamaica

St Kitts & Nevis

St Lucia

St Vincent & The Grenadines

Trinidad & Tobago

# CANADA

The present red and white maple leaf flag was adopted in 1964 and first officially flown on 15 February 1965. Red is Canada's national color and the maple leaf has been Canada's symbol since before it became a confederation in 1867. Prior to 1965, Canada's flag was red, had the Union Jack in the canton and carried the arms of Canada, which date from 1921. The shield was 'tierced in fesse,' that is, divided into three horizontal strips, with the top two divided into vertical halves containing the lions of England, the lion and tressure of Scotland, the harp of Ireland and the lilies of France—the countries from which came the people of Canada. In the lower part of the shield were the maple leaves of Canada.

*Above:* The maple leaf had been symbolic of Canada's identity for many years before this flag was officially adopted in 1964.

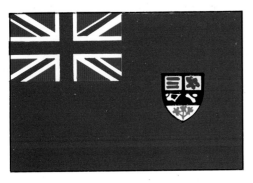

Canada (1892-1964)

Canada (1964- )

Alberta

British Columbia

Manitoba

New Brunswick

Newfoundland

Northwest Territories

Nova Scotia

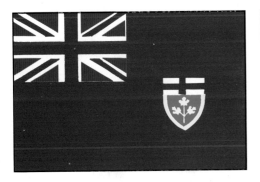

Ontario

Prince Edward Island

Quebec

Saskatchewan

Yukon Territory

# UNITED STATES
## OF
# AMERICA

Before the Continental Congress officialy adopted a flag for the United States, banners of various designs were used in the Colonies. One of the earliest Colonial flags was the Taunton Flag, which was first unfurled at Taunton, Massachusetts in 1774. It was, in reality, the Meteor Flag of England with the word 'Liberty' in large white letters across the lower part of the red field. In New England, 'Pine Tree' Flags were very popular. The pine tree was seen as symbolizing the hardiness of the New Englanders. One such design, known as the Bunker Hill Flag, which was carried by Colonial troops at the Battle of Bunker Hill on 17 June 1775, consisted of a blue field with a white canton bearing the red Cross of St George and a green pine tree. Another well-known flag consisted of a white field with a pine tree, above which were the words 'An Appeal to Heaven.' It was used by the ships of the American Navy in New England waters.

When the Revolutionary War began in 1775, there was an immediate boom in the making of flags. Massachusetts had its Pine Tree Flag, New York a black beaver on a white field, South Carolina had a handsome silver crescent on blue and Rhode Island had the blue anchor of hope. None, however, could, without arousing jealousies, be adopted as a national flag.

On 13 December 1775, there was a dinner party attended by George Washing-ton, Benjamin Franklin and other Colonial leaders. Talk turned to the flag question, and the conversation continued until Franklin made a suggestion. 'While the field of our flag must be new in the details of its design, it need not be entirely new in its elements. There is already in use a flag with which the English government is familiar, and which it has not only recognized, but also protected for more than half a century, the design of which can be readily modified, or rather extended, so as to most admirably suit our purpose. I refer to the flag of the East India Company, which is one with a field of alternate longitudinal red and white stripes and having the Cross of St George for a union.' The East India Company had been in existence for more than 150 years, and at the union of England and Scotland in 1707, the upper canton of the company's flag was changed from the Cross of St George to the union of the Crosses of St George and St Andrew. This canton was in fact the prototype of the current Union Jack.

Franklin's proposal was received with enthusiasm, and on 1 January 1776, 20 days after the dinner, Washington hoisted this national flag at Prospect Hill near Cambridge, Massachusetts. It consisted of 13 alternate red and white stripes with the Union Jack in the canton. It was variously designated as the Union Flag, the Grand Union Flag and the

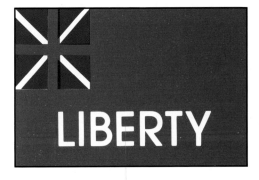

**Taunton Flag (1774)**

**Pine Tree Flag (1775)**

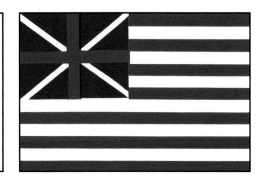

**Grand Union Flag (1776)**

**United States Flag (1776)**

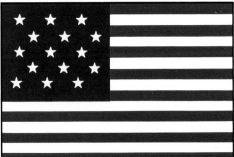

**United States Flag (1795)**

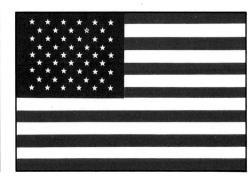

**United States Flag (1960)**

Great Union Flag, and is now occasionally referred to as the Cambridge Flag. This flag obviously had a drawback in the fact that the Union Jack was included, and as such it was not very well received. The stripes were acceptable, but there was a lot of debate over what should replace the Union Jack in the upper canton. To take away the red cross they would take away England but leave the white Cross of St Andrew, which was just as objectionable.

Perhaps one of the most compelling and enigmatic of the stories surrounding the birth of the American flag is that of Elizabeth Griscom Ross. In May 1776, Betsy Ross was approached by General Washington, who showed her a rough design of a flag with 13 stripes—like the Grand Union Flag—and 13 stars. He asked her to produce such a flag, which she did.

On 4 July 1776, four weeks later, the Continental Congress officially declared the United States to be independent of Great Britain. On 14 June 1777, the Continental Congress in Philadelphia adopted the following resolution, which established the Stars and Stripes as the official national flag: 'Resolved, That the flag of the United States be 13 stripes, alternate red and white; that the union be 13 stars,

white in a blue field representing a new constellation.'

Vermont joined the Union in 1791, and Kentucky (which was part of Virginia but later formed into a separate state, just as Tennessee was formed out of North Carolina) in 1792. There were now 15 states, so Congress declared on 15 January 1794 that 'From and after the first day of May 1795, the flag of the United States be 15 stripes and the union be 15 stars.'

The circular format, in which the stars symbolized 'union without end' was thus abandoned after being in use for 18 years. The new flag, with 15 stars, had them arranged in five horizontal rows of three each, those of the second and fourth rows being below the intervals between the others. By 1818, when five other states had been brought in and the future had others in store, it became evident that the original idea of a *stripe* as well as a star for each state would simply ruin the appearance of the flag, so on 4 April of that year, Congress decided that the number of stripes should be reduced permanently to 13, and that the union should then have 20 stars, with a new star added for each new state admitted. This flag was first flown on the House of Representatives on 13 April 1818.

After the admission of Mississippi in

1817, Illinois, Alabama, Maine, Missouri, Arkansas, Michigan, Florida and Texas were admitted during the period ending 13 May 1846, so that when the war was on that day declared against Mexico, there were 28 stars in the flag, arranged in four rows of seven each.

Six more states—Iowa, Wisconsin, California, Minnesota, Oregon and Kansas—were admitted into the Union between May 1846 and the eve of the Civil War in 1861. When the Civil War started, the stars in the flag numbered 34, arranged in five horizontal rows, with the first and second rows having seven stars each, the third row six and the fourth and fifth rows, seven stars each.

After the Civil War, the attention of the nation was turned to settling the vast area between the Missouri River and the Pacific coastal states, which was then known as the 'Wild West.' With this westward expansion came the addition of new states, and as former territories achieved statehood, new stars appeared on the flag. Nebraska, in 1867, was the first to be added on the heels of the war, and Colorado joined during the nation's centennial year in August 1876.

A major milestone in the history of the American flag came in 1889-1890, when more stars were added in a single year than at any time since the adoption of the original 13-star flag in 1777. The four states—Montana, Washington and the two Dakotas—that joined in November 1889 were followed by Idaho and Wyoming in July 1890. Together their expanse constituted an addition to the nation into which the area of the original 13 could be fitted many times over. Utah, in 1896, was the last state to join the Union in the nineteenth century.

When the twentieth century began, the area of the contiguous United States contained 45 states and four territories. In November 1907, however, the Indian Territory was officially dissolved and merged into Oklahoma as the latter achieved statehood, adding a 46th star to the flag. New Mexico and Arizona joined on 6 January and 14 February 1912, respectively, and the contiguous United States, with its 48-star flag, was complete.

By the end of the 1950s, the contiguous 48 states had been a nation for nearly half a century, but there was a

## The Stars and Bars

In 1861, when the States of the Confederacy declared their independence from the United States, they set about adopting a single national flag for the Confederate States of America, but the United States flag had 13 horizontal *stripes*, The Stars and Bars had three horizontal *bars* of red, white, red, with a large blue canton on which there was a circle of seven white stars, representing the original seven states of the Confederacy.

This circular arrangement, adopted with the old idea of all states alike—as if they each had a *particular* star—was phased out when the number of Confederate States increased to 11. This flag, known as either The Stars and Bars *or* The Southern Cross, was not a rendition of the Southern Cross constellation, as we see in the Australian flag, but rather, a blue St Andrew's Cross edged with white on a red field with stars along the arms. First flown at the Battle of Manassas in July 1861, this flag became the official Confederate *battle* flag for the rest of the war, although it was never the official *national* flag.

A form of this flag, with a broad, vertical band of red to the end of the white, and this, the fourth flag of the Confederacy, was adopted on 4 February 1865.

It was short-lived, however, as the Confederacy died at Appomattox Court House on 9 April 1865, and with it The Stars and Bars.

The motif was, however, later revived for inclusion in the Mississippi state flag.

growing statehood movement in two of the noncontiguous United States territories. Both Alaska—which was purchased from the Russian Empire in 1867—and Hawaii—which was annexed in 1898 at the urging of its citizens—now wanted to become states. There was a good deal of debate over whether to admit noncontiguous areas, but this issue seemed to be the only major stumbling block to statehood for the two territories. This was soon swept aside, and the voluminous paperwork necessary to effect the transformation began to make its way through the United States Congress and the respective state legislatures.

By the end of 1958, Alaska was ready, and on 3 January 1959, President Dwight Eisenhower officially proclaimed it the 49th State, in time for the new state's two senators and one congressman to take their seats in the 86th Congress on 6 January.

The 49-star American flag, with seven rows of seven stars, was unveiled in January and officially adopted on 4 July 1959.

It was the shortest-lived American flag in 70 years, for just six weeks later, on 21 August, President Eisenhower unveiled the 50-star flag. This, the present form of the United States flag, became official on 4 July 1960.

*Above:* **Known as 'the Stars and Stripes,' the American flag features a stripe for each of the nation's original 13 states and a star for each of the present states. There have been 50 stars since 1960.**

# THE STATE FLAGS OF

Alabama

Alaska

Arizona

Arkansas

California

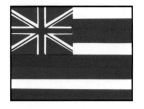

Hawaii

Idaho

Illinois

Indiana

Iowa

Massachusetts

Michigan

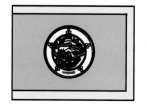

Minnesota

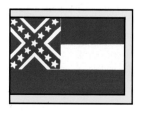

Mississippi

Missouri

New Mexico

New York

North Carolina

North Dakota

Ohio

South Dakota

Tennessee

Texas

Utah

Vermont

District of Columbia

Guam

Puerto Rico

# THE UNITED STATES

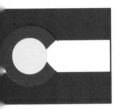
orado

Connecticut

Delaware

Florida

Georgia

nsas

Kentucky

Louisiana

Maine

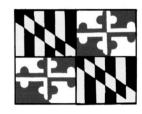
Maryland

ntana

Nebraska

Nevada

New Hampshire

New Jersey

lahoma

Oregon

Pennsylvania

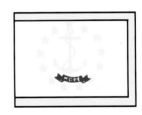
Rhode Island

South Carolina

rginia

Washington

West Virginia

Wisconsin

Wyoming

cific Islands

Virgin Islands

American Samoa

# INTERNATIONAL FLAGS

erhaps the most well-known of international flags is that of the **United Nations**, the 179-member world organization established on 24 October 1945. This flag represents a north polar view of the world with olive branches surrounding the globe. The flag flies at the United Nations headquarters in New York City and at other United Nations facilities around the world or at the site of the activities of United Nations peacekeeping forces.

The European Community (formerly European Economic Community, EEC)

or Common Market was formed on 1 July 1967 by a merger of three existing, similar organizations and is now headquartered in Brussels, Belgium. The flag of the **Council of Europe** is dark blue with a circle of gold stars representing the member nations.

The **North Atlantic Treaty Organization (NATO)** was created on 24 August 1949 as a military alliance to defend Western Europe from an attack by the Soviet Union and its Warsaw Pact allies. Both the Warsaw Pact and the Soviet Union were dissolved in 1991, but NATO

**United Nations**

**Council of Europe**

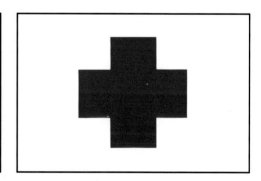
**International Red Cross**

**North Atlantic Treaty Organization (NATO)**

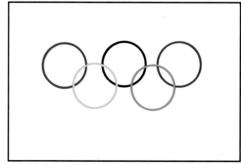
**International Olympic Committee**

remains in place as a military alliance binding Western Europe with the United States and Canada. The flag is a simple white compass rose on dark blue and flies at all NATO installations.

The flag of the **International Olympic Committee** dates to the origin of the modern Olympic Games in Athens in 1896. The flag, which flies over the Summer and Winter Games, carries five interlocking rings representing the five largest continents.

In 1863, the **International Red Cross** held an international convention in Geneva to consider how the horrors of war could be mitigated by aid to the sick and wounded. This conference proposed that in time of war, full neutrality should be granted to field and stationary hospitals, as well as to officials employed in sanitary work, volunteer nurses, civilians assisting the wounded and the wounded themselves. The conference also proposed that an identical, distinctive sign be used for medical corps of all armies, as well as an identical flag for all hospitals and ambulances and for all houses containing the wounded.

This mark was agreed to be a white flag with a red cross on it—the flag of Switzerland but reversed in color. All medical stores, carriages and the like were to bear the same device upon them, while doctors, nurses and assistants would wear a white armband with the red cross upon it, the badge that proclaimed their mission of mercy. This became the flag of the International Red Cross.

In Islamic countries, a red crescent on a white flag is substituted, and in Israel, the Star of David is used.

*Below:* **A simple blue banner, the United Nations flag features a polar view of the continents in white. The United Nations flag is similar to that of the old League of Nations that was formed after World War I, but that flag featured an oval, rather than circular, equatorial projection of the continents.**

# INDEX